Blueprints for Course Design

Blueprints for Course Design

A Learning-Centered Approach to Designing Courses, Planning Lessons, and Delivering Transformational Higher Education

JENNIFER L. BOOTH,
JOHN D. HARVEY,
MELINA W. RABON

WIPF & STOCK · Eugene, Oregon

BLUEPRINTS FOR COURSE DESIGN
A Learning-Centered Approach to Designing Courses, Planning Lessons, and Delivering Transformational Higher Education

Copyright © 2025 Jennifer L. Booth, John D. Harvey, and Melina W. Rabon. All rights reserved. Except for brief quotations in critical publications or reviews, no part of this book may be reproduced in any manner without prior written permission from the publisher. Write: Permissions, Wipf and Stock Publishers, 199 W. 8th Ave., Suite 3, Eugene, OR 97401.

Wipf & Stock
An Imprint of Wipf and Stock Publishers
199 W. 8th Ave., Suite 3
Eugene, OR 97401

www.wipfandstock.com

PAPERBACK ISBN: 979-8-3852-3561-2
HARDCOVER ISBN: 979-8-3852-3562-9
EBOOK ISBN: 979-8-3852-3563-6

VERSION NUMBER 110325

Scripture quotations taken from The Holy Bible, New International Version®, NIV®. Copyright © 2011 by Biblica, Inc. Used with permission of Zondervan. All rights reserved worldwide. www.zondervan.com

Contents

List of Contributors | vii
Introduction | ix

1. Leading the Learning: The Case for Interactive Strategies | 1
2. Know the Learner: The Differences Among Learners | 14
3. Define the Learning: The Importance of a Well-Defined Course | 39
4. Guiding the Learning: The Value of an Engaging Syllabus | 61
5. Assessing the Learning: The Rationale for Well-Designed Rubrics | 87
6. Plan the Learning: The Blueprint for a Transformational Lesson | 109
7. Facilitating the Learning: The Design of Effective Learning-Centered Tasks | 128
8. Delivering the Learning: The Opportunities of Online Learning | 148

Conclusion | 170

Appendices | 175

Bibliography | 193

List of Contributors

Jennifer L. Booth, Vice President for Enrollment Management and Retention, Columbia International University, Columbia, South Carolina

John D. Harvey, Professor of New Testament and PhD Program Director, Columbia Biblical Seminary of Columbia International University, Columbia, South Carolina

Melina W. Rabon, Associate Dean of Seminary and Professor of Practical Theology, Seminary & School of Counseling, Columbia International University, Columbia, South Carolina

Introduction

"But I learn best through lecture!" Students in a doctoral-level seminary course on Principles of Teaching, Learning, and Course Design frequently voice that sentiment when they encounter the idea of interactive learning strategies. It is an understandable sentiment, because many of them have experienced lecture as the primary modality in their previous education. They were in seminary, for instance, to learn from the theological experts on the faculty what was truly important for their future work, not to figure out for themselves what was essential for their lives and ministries, or to listen to their classmates share their (sometimes uninformed) ideas. In contrast, their experiences with discussion sessions and group projects had often been frustrating. Common problems might have been that one member of the discussion dominated the session, or that several members of the group failed to carry out their parts of the project, leaving other members to take up the slack.

Although the potential challenges of a learning-centered approach are real, the counter-question for a lecture-centered approach is, "What do you learn through lecture?" For the most part, lectures deliver content. They do little to address character and competence. In a lecture-centered approach, the instructor delivers information to students who are passive recipients of that information. It feeds the head, but it does little to make an impact on the heart or the hands. The instructor is "the sage on the stage," who dispenses his or her wisdom to the next generation of content experts.

In a learning-centered approach, the goal is learning, and the educator's role is to facilitate learning. He or she becomes "the guide on the side," while learners are active participants in the process of learning. Educators do not relinquish their "expert" status; they use it to help class members learn how to learn in ways that transform not only their knowledge but their attitudes, their behaviors, and their skills as well. (By the way, the change in language from *instructor* and *student* to *educator* and *learner* is intentional to reflect the differences in roles between the two approaches.)

As is evident from the subtitle, this book is about a learning-centered approach to designing courses, planning lessons, and delivering transformational higher education. At least four questions come to mind related to this particular attempt to encourage readers to consider using a learning-centered approach to their courses and classes.

Why Is This Book Necessary?

Many excellent educators have written excellent books on designing courses, planning lessons, and delivering education. So, why is this book necessary? It is necessary because of the focused nature of many of the other books. Multiple works address specific parts of the educational process, but few seek to address the process as a whole.

For example, Nilson's *Teaching at Its Best* touches on human factors. Wiggins and McTighe's *Understanding by Design* introduces backward design. Anderson and Krathwohl have updated and revised Bloom's taxonomy of learning objectives. Stevens and Levi have published a helpful *Introduction to Rubrics*. Harrington and Thomas suggest ways to go about *Designing a Motivational Syllabus*. Talbert's *Flipped Learning* provides a thorough discussion of that approach to lesson planning. Vella has written extensively on dialogue learning. Boettcher and Conrad's *The Online Teaching Survival Guide* addresses core principles, best practices, and tips for online teaching.

Few current works, however, take a more comprehensive approach. Wiggins and McTighe's *Understanding by Design* and Fink's *Creating Significant Learning Experiences* come the closest, although the former focuses on units within courses, and the latter omits consideration of lesson plans. Both give little attention to differences among learners, and neither gives any attention to online learning. This book seeks to fill that gap in the literature by presenting a more nearly comprehensive approach to course design and lesson planning as well as by considering the impact of online delivery on a learning-centered approach to higher education.

What Does This Book Hope to Accomplish?

This book seeks to incorporate multiple elements of educational theory and practice in order to create a comprehensive set of blueprints for the design, planning, and delivery of courses. It encourages educators in a variety of disciplines to understand, appreciate, and adopt a learning-centered approach to higher education that focuses on learners and helps them achieve measurable growth in content, character, and competence. The ultimate goal is to nurture wholistic transformation in the lives of individuals who participate in the process of learning.

A systematic approach to learning-centered education begins with a focus on knowing the learners who will be in a course. From the learners, the approach moves to course design and advocates using backward design to define the course. Backward design begins with goals and works "backward" in sequence to the units, assignments, readings, and assessments that will compose the course. A learner-friendly syllabus provides clear and organized guidance to foster engagement and enhance learning. Providing well-designed rubrics to assess assignments improves communication and reinforces course and unit goals. Lesson plans that revolve around a single big idea for each lesson and incorporate elements of flipped and dialogue learning make it possible to address multiple levels of learning as well as multiple domains of learning. Since online delivery gives access to learners who might not otherwise have the opportunity to pursue higher education through a medium that has become native to them, it is natural for a learning-centered approach to leverage an online modality to enhance learning.

The overall objective of this book is to provide a set of blueprints that educators at different levels and in different disciplines can use to design and deliver courses and classes that touch multiple aspects of learners' lives. If readers find the process understandable, logical, and practical, this book has accomplished its purpose.

Where Is This Book Going?

This book seeks to investigate the following eight operational questions:

1. What are the benefits of interactive learning?
2. What role do differences among learners play in higher education?
3. Why is it important to define a course that focuses on learning?
4. How does a learner-friendly syllabus set the tone for learning?
5. How do rubrics facilitate effective assessment of learning?
6. What are the essential components of a learning-centered lesson plan?
7. How do effective learning tasks improve engagement and encourage learning?

8. How can online courses incorporate principles of learning-centered education?

Each of the chapters seeks to address one of the operational questions. Here is an overview of the eight chapters.

Chapter 1 makes the case for interactive strategies in learning by considering the importance, purpose, benefits, and ways to address potential challenges related to a learning-centered approach.

Chapter 2 addresses the importance of understanding the differences among learners, including aspects related to memory, emotion, motivation, social and cultural dynamics, ways of receiving and processing information, and generational traits.

Chapter 3 sets out a process for defining a course, which is the necessary prelude to creating a syllabus. It argues that a learning-centered approach to course design begins with course and unit goals, considers different styles of learning, addresses three domains of learning, and aims to include three levels of learning.

Chapter 4 moves to best practices for structuring learning through syllabus design. It contends that a learning-centered approach to syllabus design provides a clear and organized framework for learning and guides learners through course expectations, objectives, and resources in a user-friendly manner.

Chapter 5 takes a learning-centered approach to assessment through the use of well-designed rubrics that support learner growth, ensure clarity of understanding, and promote continuous improvement.

Chapter 6 walks through a process for planning lessons that revolve around a simple, brief, and memorable idea, aim to address an overarching lesson goal, and use three learning spaces effectively.

Chapter 7 examines ways to facilitate learning by designing, implementing, and assessing learning tasks to improve learner engagement, academic outcomes, and meaningful learning.

Chapter 8 explores the popularity of the online modality to deliver learning and proposes that a learning-centered approach to higher education uses technology as a powerful tool for both educators and learners to enhance accessibility, engagement, and personalized learning.

Each chapter opens with a preview of the content and closes with questions for personal reflection and potential action. Chapters make extensive use of tables, graphics, and examples. Appendices provide templates to use, and a bibliography lists resources for additional reference and study.

Whom Does This Book Hope to Serve?

This book hopes both to serve and to challenge active and aspiring educators in all disciplines who are interested in increasing the effectiveness of the learning that takes place in their courses, programs, and organizations. Because it sets out a consistent approach to course design, lesson planning, and online delivery, it should appeal to educators who teach courses in different modalities. Because it provides a systematic method for applying that approach, it should appeal to learners and educators in a variety of disciplines and settings. Because it builds on previous work by Wiggins and McTighe (backward design), Fink (integrated design), Bloom (educational objectives), Talbert (flipped learning), and Vella (dialogue learning) among others, it should interest professional educators. Hopefully, this book will serve a variety of educators in a variety of ways and in so doing will enhance the growth of the learners with whom those educators work.

Not a Conclusion but a Beginning

The conclusion of this introduction is not the end of the conversation. Indeed, it is the beginning of one. The ensuing conversation might challenge some of the preconceptions of some readers, and it might confirm some of the preconceptions of other readers. If it does either—or both—it is a conversation that is worth having. A good starting point would be to take a few minutes to reflect on the Food for Thought questions below. Take advantage of the opportunity to reflect, and then, join the conversation.

Food for Thought
What has been the main approach to learning that you have experienced in your educational journey?
What have been some situations in which you have experienced interactive learning?
What did you see as benefits of interactive learning? What did you see as challenges?
What initial questions do you have about a learning-centered approach to education?

1

Leading the Learning: The Case for Interactive Strategies

Chapter Preview
A learning-centered approach to course design considers the purpose, potential challenges, and benefits of interactive learning.
Essential questions to answer in understanding the importance of a learning-centered course are: (1) Why is a learning-centered approach more effective than traditional approaches? (2) What are the benefits of implementing this approach? (3) What are the potential challenges and solutions to implementing learning-centered strategies?
The key to understanding a learning-centered approach is awareness of the paradigm shift from the educator to the learner as the major participant in the learning process.
By taking responsibility for their learning, class members enhance engagement, critical thinking, metacognition, and content retention, resulting in a greater ability to apply knowledge and reflect on their lives and ministries.

THE GOAL IS LEARNING, and the most effective way for educators to lead learning is to include interactive strategies in their courses. All educators are responsible to their institutions for engaging learners in the process of learning. Christian faculty members, however, have a deeper accountability to God. Their calling includes providing cognitive knowledge of the subject material, but Jesus never intended his followers to grasp only "a simple knowledge about the Bible. . . . As the New Testament unfolds, growing to maturity represents a major objective."[1] Paul instructed pastor-teachers "to equip [God's] people for works of service, so that the body of Christ may be built up until we all reach unity in the faith and in the knowledge of the Son of God and become mature, attaining to the whole measure of the fullness of Christ" (Eph 4:12–13, NIV). The call to equip God's people for service is both a challenge and a means toward spiritual maturity. Educators, therefore, must remain vigilant in developing skills that will serve learners more effectively. One way to equip, engage, and serve them is to consider a more learning-centered rather than a teacher-centered approach to education.[2]

Why Choose a Learning-Centered Approach?

Plutarch, the first-century Greek philosopher and writer, observed, "The mind does not require filling like a bottle, but rather, like wood, it only requires kindling to create in it an impulse to think independently and an ardent desire for the truth."[3] He believed that learning is more than "filling" students' heads with facts and concepts. Instead, the teacher's responsibility is to "kindle" or stir within students the desire to engage and wrestle with the information and ideas that will produce meaningful and lifelong learning. Plutarch was advocating for what educators call a more learning-centered strategy for education.

Proponents of a learning-centered method of teaching conclude that "students learn more and retain their knowledge longer if they acquire it in an active rather than a passive manner."[4] In this book active learning refers to "any instructional [strategy] that engages students in the learning process, in an active way, as part of the group space activities."[5] The activities can be presentations, debates, case studies, or problem-solving discussions. When educators intentionally integrate these types of activities

---

1. Lawson, *Professor's Puzzle*, 26–27.
2. Portions of this chapter are adapted from Rabon, "Teaching Strategies."
3. Plutarch, *De auditu*, 258–59.
4. Fink, *Guide to Designing Courses*, 16.
5. Talbert, *Flipped Learning*, 12.

into curriculum design, they deepen understanding, increase retention, and promote spiritual transformation.

Effective teaching strategies often involve "integrating concrete and abstract knowledge acquired through active and passive methods of learning."[6] Although teaching assessments demonstrate that learners tend to learn best through active learning, many professors still rely on lectures and value them as an effective approach for delivering comprehensive content or explaining complex topics. Even though evidence suggests that class members retain relatively little from lectures, professors in higher education continue to use it as their most common method of conveying content. Graham notes that relying solely on "treating students as passive recipients of knowledge is not very effective in producing people who truly live the Christian life. It only produces people who can talk about it in someone else's language."[7] In other words, passive learning often leads to a shallow comprehension of the subject matter. Educators, therefore, must explore additional strategies to enhance engagement, motivation, and transformation. Those strategies will foster deeper knowledge and more authentic application of learning to life and ministry.

There are times when a lecture is of value to students (i.e., defining key terms, introducing concepts, summarizing content). An integrative method of teaching can work if educators shorten their lecture time and include more active teaching strategies to prevent disengagement from the learning process. Lectures tend to be a one-way conversation in which learners have "no direct contact with the subject, are unable to investigate, explore, or judge [it] for themselves."[8] If lecture is the only method used during a lesson, sustaining class members' attention can be difficult. Using a more balanced approach that incorporates active and passive teaching strategies maximizes the strengths of both methods.

Most students prefer active learning. For that reason, Levine writes that educators must teach in ways that are "consistent with the ways our students learn most effectively. It means that the curriculum must meet our students where they are, not where we hope they might be or where we are."[9] In other words, learners do not need to change; educators should design their courses to align with how students learn best.

To engage students, educators need to forgo the "transmission model." This model focuses on "what the teacher does rather than on what the

---

6. Levine and Dean, *Generation on a Tightrope*, 185.
7. Graham, *Teaching Redemptively*, 71.
8. Kolb and Kolb, *Experiential Educator*, xxv.
9. Levine and Dean, *Generation on a Tightrope*, 168–69.

students are supposed to learn."[10] In the learning-centered model, the "importance of the learner outweighs the content to be learned, the teacher who facilitates learning, or the process by which content is communicated."[11] Surveys confirm that lecture does not help class members "retain information after a course is over, develop an ability to transfer knowledge to novel situations, develop skill in thinking or problem solving, [or] achieve affective outcomes, such as motivation for additional learning or a change in attitude."[12] Learners are unlikely to retain factual knowledge over the long term without effective reinforcement strategies. Information "rapidly deteriorates unless the ideas can be meaningfully encoded or practiced with some regularity. When students think about material in more meaningful ways, underlying brain structures will change to promote more enduring learning."[13] Newton notes that educators can "unknowingly inhibit the brain's learning ability by teaching in an ultralinear, structured, and predictable fashion. The result is bored or frustrated learners."[14] Consequently, there is a disconnect between what class members favor and what many faculty members prefer.

Educators must recognize that engaging and transforming learners requires designing courses with a more learning-centered and active approach to education. Students, rather than the teacher, become the central figures of the class. Class members desire to "do" something active in the classroom. A Barnes and Noble survey of students in higher education revealed that 50.5 percent preferred learning by doing (e.g., working through examples), 37.6 percent favored learning by seeing (e.g., reading course materials), and only 11.9 percent preferred learning by listening (e.g., lectures).[15] To make an impact on learners in all three domains of learning—cognitive, affective, and behavioral—a more active approach is essential. Advocates of a more active approach to learning emphasize a fundamental point: teaching is more than telling.

---

10. Bain, *Best College Teachers*, 48.

11. Yount, *Created to Learn*, 53.

12. Fink, *Significant Learning Experiences*, 3. See also Sousa, *How the Brain Learns*, 106.

13. McKeachie and Svinicki, *Teaching Tips*, 319.

14. Newton, *Heart-Deep Teaching*, 114–15.

15. Barnes and Noble College, *Getting to Know Gen Z*, 8.

What Are the Benefits of a Learning-Centered Approach?

Using a learning-centered approach has multiple benefits. First, it is *holistic*. Actively engaging learners in the learning process promotes deeper knowledge acquisition, fosters personal growth, and leads to spiritual transformation. Strawser writes that learning is a holistic endeavor to transform not only the mind but "perspectives, habits of mind, mind-sets, [and] mental models . . . so that [the students] may generate beliefs and opinions that will prove more true or justified to guide action."[16] In other words, to educate, equip, and transform learners, higher education must do more than transfer information. Educators must engage students in ways that shape their intellect, mature their spirit, and lead to action. Maturity, however, cannot occur if learners struggle to focus and educators fail to capture their attention. For Christian faculty members, engaging the learner becomes a godly responsibility, because the purpose of education goes beyond merely acquiring biblical knowledge to changing learners' lives and teaching them to love God and others more completely.

Second, a learning-centered approach is *engaging*. It promotes meaningful dialogue and encourages class members to connect with the material in greater depth. Disengagement, often a symptom of lecture-heavy courses, hinders academic success and creates a deficiency in future vocational and life preparation. Learners enjoy hands-on experiences that place them in the heart of the learning process, rather than just on the sidelines as observers. For example, preparing and teaching a Bible study lesson, rather than merely receiving instruction on how to facilitate one, equips class members with practical skills that go beyond theory. In contrast, courses that rely heavily on lectures often fail to maintain attention and lead to disengagement. By using a learning-centered approach, educators can engage learners more effectively and can promote intellectual, spiritual, and vocational growth.

Third, a learning-centered approach is *focused*. It enhances learners' ability to retain information by aligning teaching strategies with how the brain processes and stores knowledge. Attention is a crucial component in learning. If class members maintain focus, attention increases and prolongs neural brain activity. The sensory and conceptual neurons reach the prefrontal cortex and promote long-term retention in a process called long-term potentiation. For example, if learners pay conscious attention to specific content, there is a higher chance that material will move from their

---

16. Strawser, *Transformative Student Experiences*, 2.

short-term to long-term memory. Studies of the brain reveal that the ability to pay attention includes the choice to ignore other stimuli. The result is "selective attention." Unfortunately, educators must battle for the brain's attention against an ever-increasing number of external and internal distractions in the classroom.

Fourth, a learning-centered approach is *developmental*. By emphasizing self-reflection and problem-solving it aids in the development of metacognition skills and critical thinking abilities, helping learners take ownership of their learning. Metacognition is "a learner's ability to monitor, reflect on, and improve on his or her learning activities and strategies, a key factor in successful transfer of knowledge and skills to new learning situations."[17] Students learn to think about thinking, thus reaching deeper levels of contemplation. Metacognition skills are especially important for learners who have grown up with the external stimuli of a screen telling them what to think, rather than developing their own internal convictions. Class members need to become experts in owning their learning. When they become responsible for their learning, they realize "a great education does [not] come from a teacher who thinks for you, it comes from a teacher who nudges you to think for yourself."[18]

Fifth, a learning-centered approach is *integrative*. Learners who are actively engaged have greater potential for learning the content, effectively relating what they learn to the overall objectives of the class, connecting the content to prior learning, and applying their learning to real-life situations. Active teaching strategies decrease their dependence on the educator and increase self-regulated learning. The educator becomes the interpreter, coach, and guide, not the informer and protector of knowledge. The learner becomes personally involved and fully engaged in discovering, exploring, and interpreting the meaning of the content rather than passively listening.

Sixth, a learning-centered approach is *collaborative*. God created his people for relationship and connection. Education provides an opportunity to use these connections to foster meaningful learning. A key aspect of an andragogical strategy is learner-to-learner interaction, which promotes a more holistic learning experience. Classmates are a valuable asset in encouraging spiritual formation in one another and in supporting each other in the learning process. This type of strategy in the classroom is particularly crucial because, as Elmore and McPeak note, "More Americans shop alone, dine alone, and live alone than those who do so with family or friends."[19]

---

17. Taylor and Marienau, *Facilitating Learning*, 198.
18. Elmore and McPeak, *Marching off the Map*, 121.
19. Elmore and McPeak, *Marching off the Map*, 257.

Countless hours of isolation on devices have significantly hindered many students emotionally and relationally. Learners who learn how to cooperate, collaborate, and engage with each other develop essential relational skills. Building community is vital in education because these experiences with others not only enhance learning but also foster spiritual transformation through meaningful relationships.

Finally, a learning-centered approach is *reinforcing*. When educators use learning-centered strategies, class members receive immediate feedback and opportunities for self-assessment, which reinforces understanding. A key advantage to learning-centered approaches is the ability to hear feedback and ongoing assessment of understanding in the classroom. As class members engage in discussion, ask questions, reflect, and relate the content to their experiences, the educator can evaluate their comprehension of the material presented in class. Immediate assessment has the advantage of helping educators address any misunderstandings instantaneously. Furthermore, gathering feedback and assessment in the classroom assists the educator in determining whether additional content might enhance the level of learners' understanding of that content and its relevance for their lives.

The following table summarizes key benefits of a learning-centered approach to education:

Holistic	Promotes deeper knowledge acquisition, personal growth, and spiritual transformation.
Engaging	Promotes meaningful dialogue and encourages learners to connect with the material in greater depth.
Focused	Enhances the ability to retain information in both short-term and long-term memory.
Developmental	Aids in the development of learners' metacognition skills and critical thinking abilities.
Integrative	Relates learning to course objectives, prior learning, and real-life situations.
Collaborative	Provides an opportunity to use relationships and connections to foster meaningful learning.
Reinforcing	Provides immediate feedback and opportunities for self-assessment to reinforce understanding.

In the discussion of the preceding benefits, three factors deserve fuller consideration: focus, metacognition skills, and collaborative learning.

Why Are Focus, Metacognition, and Collaboration Important?

The internet and digital devices have made it increasingly difficult for educators to sustain *focus*. Bunce, Flens, and Neiles report that learners experience "attention lapses as early as the first 30 [seconds] of a lecture with the next lapse occurring approximately 4.5 minutes into a lecture and again at shorter and shorter cycles throughout the lecture."[20] Wilmer, Sherman, and Chein note that class members who lack focus do not have "the capacity to attend to only one source of information while ignoring other incoming stimuli. Focused attention encompasses sustained attention—the ability to maintain a directed attentional focus over an extended period of time."[21] Some learners exhibit a "hyper attention" that causes their brains to adapt and shift constantly between objects of focus. Even if class members do not touch the phone, the "ping" or "vibration" disrupts their attentiveness in class and in completing class assignments. Many college-age young people confess that the phone is a distraction because they are bored.

Among members of Gen Z, born between 1995 and 2012, smartphones are the number-one distraction when they are completing assignments. Most of them check their phones every thirty minutes or less. In blocked classes, class members engage their digital devices every five to six minutes on average. Gen Zers admit that their smartphones divert their attention multiple times for non-class activities such as texting, scrolling, or watching videos. Even class members who do not use their phones find it difficult to concentrate when classmates are on their devices. Unless institutions ban phones from class, class members will continue to bring them and shift their attention away from learning.

Despite these challenges, educators can design engaging courses that cultivate and sustain attention. Diverting learners' attention toward more rigorous cognitive work is a challenge. In order to succeed, educators must shift their strategy "from preventing distraction and toward cultivating attention."[22] Consequently, they need to come alongside learners to help "combat over-stimulated, over-taxed, over-connected, over-committed, [and] overwhelmed lifestyles."[23] The necessity of finding creative ways to make in-class time more compelling becomes an increasingly important part of educational strategies. The good news is that although smartphone

---

20. Bunce et al., "How Long Can Students," 1442.
21. Wilmer et al., "Smartphones and Cognition," 4.
22. Lang, *Distracted*, 15.
23. Elmore and McPeak, *Marching off the Map*, 228.

usage might have an impact on cognitive tasks, there is not enough evidence currently to understand the long-term effects on attentional functioning. In other words, learners are capable of sustained attention.

Ultimately, learners bear the responsibility for remaining focused in class. Educators, however, must understand that class members come to class with external and internal distractions. Adopting learning-centered strategies to grab their attention is essential to meaningful learning. Creating more effective and transformative courses that captivate learners' attention is critical to their success in the cognitive, affective, and behavioral domains of learning. A learning-centered approach can help circumvent some of the distractions and encourage class members to refocus and connect in the classroom. It not only redirects attention in the classroom, it also cultivates habits such as self-monitoring and reflection—skills that employers recognize as essential for workplace success.

The National Association of Colleges and Educators reports that employers value *metacognition skills*. They state that "the top-rated career readiness competencies continue to be communication, teamwork, and critical thinking skills."[24] Exceptional educators prioritize helping learners "evaluate how they think and behave beyond the classroom"[25] over merely preparing them to pass an exam.

To help learners develop these skills and characteristics, professors in higher education institutions must shift from the traditional pedagogical approach to a more andragogical approach. Unlike pedagogy, andragogy focuses on the process of problem-solving and experience rather than on content and explanation. An andragogical approach allows class members to take responsibility for their education, while the educator serves as a resource rather than the central figure in the class. The principles guiding the lesson encompass the learners' experiences, and the discovery of how the content addresses those experiences creates an intrinsic motivation for class members to study and apply the knowledge they acquire.

In today's fast-paced, technology-driven world, learners often lack the skills to think critically, which is a vital component of the andragogical approach. For instance, emotional reasoning, a more subjective path to determine what is real or valid, is increasingly replacing objective critical thinking.[26] Although learners are adept at using technology, they might lack the analytical skills necessary to evaluate the vast amount of information they encounter each day. Adopting a more active approach to learning

---

24. Gatta et al., *Job Outlook 2024*, 6.
25. Bain, *Best College Teachers*, 94.
26. Zarra, *Entitled Generation*, 18.

encourages them to develop the metacognitive and critical thinking skills they need to discern fact from fiction and to apply their knowledge in meaningful ways.

Cross writes that learners who experience *collaborative learning* in the classroom are more "satisfied with their educational experience . . . and perceive themselves to have learned more than students who are less involved with the people and activities of the college."[27] Participation in discussions, projects, debates, or other cooperative activities creates opportunities for creativity, communication, collaboration, and deeper critical thinking in the classroom.

Several educators refer to Mezirow's transformative learning theory, which "highlights not just 'real learning' but suggest[s] that through the process of self-reflection and engagement with others, complete personal transformation occurs."[28] Group activities and one-on-one discussions or any activity centered around "the social dimension, more than any other, has contributing value to one's spiritual development and growth."[29] Connections with others matter and affect "how we learn, relate to others, and navigate an increasingly networked society."[30]

Building on the importance of learner engagement and collaboration, chapter 7 will examine several teaching strategies that faculty members can incorporate into their lessons to enhance participation and involvement in the learning process. The more class members engage in the learning process, the greater the likelihood they will value and connect with the content. Active learning moves learners sequentially toward deeper levels of problem solving and cognitive development.

What Are the Potential Challenges of a Learning-Centered Approach?

Despite the benefits of a learning-centered approach, the strategy also has its challenges. Educators might question whether including an additional component justifies the *extra time and effort* required to revise their lesson plans. They might think that an increase in learning-centered strategies means a decrease in content coverage, which equals a reduction in learning. Although they might cover less content than in traditional lectures, the material they present is more easily encoded by the brain when it is

27. Cross, *Making Connections*, 18.
28. Lowe and Lowe, *Ecologies of Faith*, 84.
29. Lowe and Lowe, *Ecologies of Faith*, 130.
30. Lowe and Lowe, *Ecologies of Faith*, 133.

combined with active strategies, and allows the information to move into long-term memory. The goal of learning is to deposit the information in long-term memory so that class members can recall and apply what they have learned in daily life, work, and ministry situations. Although learning-centered activities might require additional time, it does not necessarily follow that adding these components will hinder the course goals or reduce understanding of the material. These additional activities can enhance both retention and the application of the knowledge gained.

To address this concern, one effective approach is to start with minor changes, integrating one active learning task into a lesson instead of overhauling the entire curriculum plan. As educators become more comfortable with incorporating a learning-centered approach, they can gradually increase the level of activity over time, rather than making extensive changes all at once. The key is to concentrate on meeting lesson goals instead of covering extensive amounts of content that students probably will not remember. The motto "less is more" gives learners time to reflect, which in turn improves retention and application for life and career.

Another potential drawback to using more active strategies is *lack of participation*. Class members who are more introverted might feel anxious or fearful to speak in class. A learner's hesitancy to participate can also derive from fear of giving a wrong answer or expressing one with which others might disagree. Part of the hesitancy to speak up comes from a desire to be safe and avoid the risk of their professor or peers judging them. Anxious feelings or a perception of judgmental attitudes can potentially hinder academic performance, cause a lack of engagement in learning activities, or inhibit collaboration with classmates.

To alleviate this fear, assure class members that the class will consider all perspectives and questions. Learners need encouragement to take the risk of asking or answering questions and to see the value in hearing someone else's perspective or interpretations, even if the response might be incorrect. Another strategy to reduce fear is to promote curiosity and to prioritize effort over correct answers. Classes can utilize online polls, enabling students to submit answers anonymously or discuss questions with a partner before participating in a larger class discussion. These approaches help reduce the anxiety of responding on the spot, allowing class members the time to reflect on their responses without feeling the pressure to respond publicly. Allowing learners to choose their discussion partners can reduce the discomfort of talking to people whom they do not know. These strategies create an environment where class members feel more confident and willing to participate in class activities. Finally, the educator should affirm the unique gifts and talents that each class member contributes to the class, reinforcing their value throughout the semester. Bain notes that the best teachers "look for and appreciate the individual value of each student [because] every student is unique and brings contributions that no one else can make."[31]

Some teachers, however, might fear that learning-centered strategies could lead to *off-topic discussions* during group activities. Creating a space for open discussion is important, and staying on topic is essential for effective group work and meaningful outcomes. One of the goals in any discussion is to help class members maintain focus on the subject, enabling them to contribute to the learning process. The key to circumventing off-topic conversations is to present learners with clear, detailed instructions, time constraints, and expectations that align with the activity. These guidelines help prevent digressions from the topic and ensure the group work remains productive and relevant to the subject matter.

There might be times when educators require class members to read or watch material before participating in an activity. Learners, unfortunately, have a reputation for *not completing outside assignments* before class. To help alleviate this problem, clearly connect pre-class assignments to in-class activities to help class members see the value of the work outside of class. Requiring graded application or reflection papers before class or incorporating short quizzes on the main points of the content can also motivate learners to complete the assignment. An additional approach is to ask several class members to teach portions of the pre-assignment material or lead discussions on the content. By combining these strategies, educators encourage class members to engage the material ahead of time and also foster a sense of ownership, making the learning process more meaningful.

The following table summarizes the preceding potential challenges and possible ways to address those challenges:

Extra time and effort	Incorporate active learning tasks incrementally on a lesson-by-lesson basis over time.
Lack of student participation	Create a learning environment that values each student's contribution.
Off-topic discussions	Provide detailed instructions, time constraints, and expectations that align with the learning activity.
Incomplete assignments	Connect pre-class assignments to in-class activities and to course grading.

---

31. Bain, *Best College Teachers*, 72.

Conclusion

Professors in higher education institutions must move from the teaching-centered approach to a learning-centered approach. Learning-centered strategies encourage class members to take responsibility for their learning, as the educator guides and fosters engagement, reflection, analysis, and application of the subject material. A more active, learning-centered approach is not only what many learners prefer; it can also provide the motivation to push them toward deeper levels of learning. Active experiences navigate learners toward deeper knowledge, behaviors, and skills, producing spiritually mature Christians who are prepared to continue to know Christ and make him known.

Food for Thought
In what ways might you intentionally design your courses to integrate the key benefits of a learning-centered approach to ensure both academic rigor and meaningful student engagement?
What are some ways in which you can design engaging courses that cultivate and sustain learners' attention while also increasing the metacognition skills?
What institutional, educational, or logistical challenges might arise when you shift from a transmission-based model to a more learning-centered approach?
What are practical first steps that you could take to align your instruction to the way in which class members learn most effectively?

2

Know the Learner: The Differences Among Learners

Chapter Preview
A learning-centered approach examines the cognitive and contextual aspects that influence learners' engagement with course content.
Essential questions to answer in understanding the learner include: (1) What cognitive and contextual factors should educators consider when designing a course? (2) How can they build meaningful connections with learners? (3) What are some practical strategies that facilitate better understanding of learners?
Understanding class members as holistic learners is essential for meaningful learning. By examining the differences among learners, educators can create environments that motivate them toward more meaningful learning.

THE GOAL IS LEARNING, and in order for meaningful learning to take place, educators must first capture learners' attention. They ignite interest and curiosity by creating environments conducive to learning. A clear understanding of learners' characteristics and needs enables educators to create optimal learning environments, select effective teaching strategies, and design appropriate course content. Prioritizing learners' needs over the educator's preferences challenges a one-size-fits-all approach. Each class of learners is unique and requires educators to reassess the course, even when the subject matter remains the same. Effective educators understand that they "do [not] teach a class. [They] teach a student."[1] Studies consistently show that learners desire "their teachers to be interested in them as persons, and those educators who are, amplify the impact of their teaching."[2] Educators who first engage their learners personally can then engage them academically.

Most learners attend class expecting to gain knowledge in their field of study, but they cannot learn if they are not engaged. Chapter 1 discussed why it is important to use engaging learning strategies. This chapter explores the importance of knowing the learner as one of the ways of establishing engagement. What follows is an overview of how people learn and how those learning processes affect retention of knowledge, acquisition of skills, and transformation of behavior. First, however, it is necessary to clarify the definition of learning. Learning is an active process that results in lasting changes in a learner's knowledge, attitudes, and skills. A class member who crams the night before an exam and merely recalls information for the test is not learning. Real learning requires the ability to transfer knowledge beyond the classroom. Learners must actively engage with content, reflect on it, and receive proper guidance in applying what they learn to real-world situations. Educators play a vital role in guiding learners through the transformational process of growing in their knowledge, attitude, and skill over time.

One of the most effective ways to enhance classroom learning is by recognizing the unique contributions each learner brings to the learning environment. A learning-centered approach places learners at the center of the learning process, valuing their perspectives and experiences. Educators who adopt a learning-centered mindset intentionally design courses and assignments that align with class members' needs, interests, learning styles, and abilities rather than relying only on their assumptions of what is best. These educators begin with the assumption that learners have both the ability and the desire to learn, and a learning-centered approach recognizes the importance of a deeper understanding of their learners. The way class members learn dictates the curricular design of the course. Jane Vella notes that "when there is nothing in a course . . . that speaks directly to the learner, he or she will not learn."[3] The educator's goal is to aim for authentic engagement, which only happens when the learner sees the "immediate value in what they are learning, and [is] motivated to pursue their new learning

1. Baker, *Integration of Abilities*, xiii.
2. Bain, *Best College Teachers*, 30.
3. Vella, *On Teaching and Learning*, 95.

beyond the classroom."[4] Class members engage when content is relevant and applicable to their lives, and educators achieve relevance only through intentional efforts to know the learner.

The following sections highlight six key aspects of learners that assist educators in gaining a deeper understanding of the ways in which those aspects influence the thinking, behavior, and engagements of learners:

1. Memory
2. Emotion
3. Motivation
4. Cultural and Social Dynamics
5. Receiving and Processing Information
6. Generational Traits

Understanding and applying these aspects will enable educators to design more effective classes and courses that better support their learners and enrich the learning experience. Although it is not an exhaustive treatment of every subject related to the learner, the following discussion includes essential topics and characteristics helpful in understanding and knowing learners.

Aspects Related to Memory

Most class members arrive in class with digital devices that demand a significant share of their cognitive attention. Smartphones, especially, can produce gaps in learners' cognitive, affective, and psychomotor domains. These devices are rewiring their brains. Technology reshapes attention, increases distraction, reduces sustained focus, and causes a reduction in interest in non-screen experiences. Teaching becomes the art of "creating conditions [and environments] that lead to change in a learner's brain."[5] Understanding how the brain processes, retains, and retrieves information helps educators design courses that align with learners' cognitive abilities and counteract some of the neural rewiring caused by the overuse of digital devices.

Neuroscientists call the "persistent wiring and reshaping of brain circuits caused by environmental input as neuroplasticity. Learning, then is the epitome of neuroplasticity."[6] As class members encounter new material,

---

4. Sousa, *Rewired Brain*, 16.
5. Zull, *Changing the Brain*, 5.
6. Sousa, *Rewired Brain*, 25.

their brains adapt and change. As class members hear new information and cultivate new skills, the neural pathways charge and connect to one another, preserving the learning and recall of the material. Engaging in meaningful learning literally transforms the learners' brains. The brain's capacity for change is encouraging, but the greatest challenge might not be the brain's ability to learn, but its ability to focus. Chapter 1 addressed the topic of attention and distraction as they relate to learning, but it is helpful to review the topic briefly as it relates specifically to brain function and cognitive processing.

Unfortunately, time in front of screens hardwires the brain to process information at a hyperactive pace. The issue does not lie in a diminished capacity for attention itself, but rather in the reduction of time individuals are willing to spend on a particular task. Because of technology, the brain's neural pathways have become conditioned to anticipate rapid shifts in stimuli, making it more difficult for individuals to sustain attention in learning environments that do not constantly change. Since learners encounter a steady influx of sensory input, their brains filter out anything they deem irrelevant or boring in order to focus on what they believe matters. Educational theorists call this process the primacy-recency effect, which is the brain's tendency to prioritize information that is relevant or novel over material seen as unconnected or insignificant to them personally.[7] Understanding the memory process brings an increased awareness of why some information becomes a permanent part of learners' knowledge while other information is quickly forgotten. This awareness helps educators know what to include or exclude in their courses.

When educators introduce new material, the goal is to move the information into the brain's long-term memory. Understanding the process of memory helps the educator understand why learners remember some material while they forget other content. The first step in the process is *the input of sensory information* that the brain holds for less than a second. During this valuable second, the brain engages the second step—*the attention filter*—to determine what it will or will not do with the information. If the brain decides to disregard the information, the learning process does not move forward. Educators have to convince class members that "they want to learn something (e.g., because it is fascinating), need to learn something (e.g., because it is useful), or feel they should learn something (e.g., because I will help someone else)."[8] When the brain encounters content that appears

---

7. Sousa, *Rewired Brain*, 54.
8. Goodwin and Marzano, *New Classroom Instruction*, 32.

relevant or activates curiosity, it transfers the information into short-term or working memory.

In the third step, *the working memory* analyzes, compares, and connects new information with prior knowledge. When learners find the new information interesting and relevant to their future, the brain stores the information. The working memory, however, can only handle a limited amount of information (about four to seven items for adults) and only holds it for a short time (averaging five to ten minutes for young people, and ten to twenty minutes for adults). When educators present too much information, the working memory becomes overloaded, and the attention span begins to short-circuit. The brain is "essentially lazy, always eager to revert back to 'low-effort mode'" in order to conserve energy rather than engage in sustained effort.[9] Therefore, educators should avoid overwhelming class members with excessive content in a brief period of time. To facilitate memory, therefore, less is more.

Educators who understand the brain's memory process and who know their learners can more effectively discern what is relevant or irrelevant to them. Engagement increases when the material connects to knowledge, attitudes, or skills that support future application. Furthermore, educators should focus on presenting critical points of the lesson at the beginning of class when attention runs highest and should return to them at the end of class when attention spikes again. Configuring class time in this way "causes the brain to put forth effort to attach sense and meaning to the new learning, make connections to past learning, mentally summarize, and internalize the new learning."[10] Understanding how the working memory functions helps educators choose what to include or exclude during class. Chapter 7 will outline a practical class schedule that aligns with how the brain processes memory.

The fourth step in moving information to long-term memory is *encoding*, where the brain "convert[s] the information from one form of electrical impulses (sensory input) into a new set of electrical patterns (memories)."[11] In other words, now the learner makes sense of the material by relating the new content to prior knowledge or experience and organizes it in a meaningful way for retrieval later. The practical implication for educators is to include reflection and application exercises into the lesson plan to help class members move to the next step in the process.

---

9. Kahneman, quoted in Goodwin and Marzano, *New Classroom Instruction*, 64.
10. Sousa, *Rewired Brain*, 64.
11. Goodwin and Marzano, *New Classroom Instruction*, 61.

In the fifth step, the brain begins the process of *consolidation* to integrate and interpret the new information, thus strengthening and stabilizing the connections between the new and preexisting knowledge. When learners think about and personalize what they are learning, they are more likely to recall and remember it. Consolidation occurs both at night, while a person sleeps, and during the day through repeated practice and retrieval of information. Learners who spend hours on smartphones, however, can weaken the brain's ability to encode and consolidate information. Introducing a no-phone policy in the classroom gives class members' brains a chance to rest from digital distractions. To support consolidation, educators can also stress the importance of a good night's sleep. Although they cannot control how much their learners sleep, educators can structure class to include repetition, retrieval, and screen-free engagement practices to increase neural connections and reduce information loss.

Once consolidated, the sixth step moves the information into *long-term memory*, where the brain stores the data for future retrieval and application. Unlike working memory, which has a limited storage capacity, long-term memory has a virtually limitless capacity. Long-term memory is where the brain retains information indefinitely for future use. The key implication for educators is to emphasize practice, practice, and more practice. Practice, however, does not mean rote memorization. Effective practice involves engagement with the content in different contexts, strengthening connections and enhancing understanding. For example, students who are learning a language might initially memorize vocabulary, but deeper learning occurs when they practice speaking, reading, or writing in the language. Repeated and purposeful practice helps the brain encode information. Allowing time between classes for consolidation leads to greater retention and mastery of the material. One effective technique is distributed, or spaced, practice. Learners practice what they learn immediately in class and continue to revisit the material over intervals of time, either in or outside of class, resulting in more meaningful and sustained learning.

The seventh and final step is to *recall* the knowledge when retrieval is necessary. The stored information returns to conscious awareness, so that the learner can promptly apply it when needed. Long-term memory retrieval becomes more efficient when learners encode information that is emotionally engaging, personally relevant, and repeated over time. The following table summarizes the seven steps in the memory process:

Memory Process Steps		
1	Sensory Input	Reception of information through the senses
2	Attention Filter	Identification of relevant information
3	Working Memory	Connection of information to prior knowledge
4	Encoding	Organization of information for storage
5	Consolidation	Transfer of information to long-term storage
6	Long-Term Memory	Retention of information for future use
7	Recall	Retrieval of information when needed

Aspects Related to Emotion

Although repetition and cognitive effort contribute to learning, meaningful learning is nearly impossible without the involvement of emotion. The portion of the brain that processes emotions determines whether new information is worth preserving.[12] In other words, if the content is emotionally neutral, the brain rarely stores it. Conversely, if the subject is emotionally significant, the learner is more likely to remember the material.

Emotions, whether good or bad, influence the information a learner chooses to engage during class. When there are positive emotions, such as excitement or curiosity, the brain shifts to discovery mode. Engagement increases and heightens the chance that the information makes its way to learners' long-term memory. When there are negative emotions, such as anxiety or fear, the brain shifts to defensive mode. Attention decreases, and the learning process suffers. The key is to remember that "emotions drive attention and attention drives learning."[13]

Emotions are important when considering how to plan and implement course material. The strength of emotions can influence the learner's attention, retention, and recall. The weaker the emotions, the less chance there is that the brain will store the information in long-term memory. Educators need to consider how class members might feel about a topic, because

---

12. Sousa, *Rewired Brain*, 56–57.
13. Sousa, *Rewired Brain*, 19.

"how [they] feel influences how [they] think."[14] In other words, emotional responses shape their cognitive processing.

To support deeper learning and recall, educators need to be intentional about cultivating pleasurable emotions, such as joy, humor, hope, gratitude, empathy, and awe within the classroom. When educators model these types of emotions, they can activate corresponding emotional responses in learners, thereby increasing engagement and a willingness to learn. Research in affective neuroscience indicates that when a lesson elicits strong emotions, it initiates physiological and cognitive processes that increase focus, activate relevant memories, stimulate decision-making, and foster creative thinking. These emotional responses result in knowledge that is meaningful and applicable to the learners' real-life context. Conversely, knowledge disconnected from emotional relevance discourages motivation and engagement. As a result, triggering emotional curiosity not only enhances engagement but sustains motivation to continue learning.

Curiosity prompts learners to ask new questions, seek deeper insights, and pursue additional knowledge beyond the classroom. These positive emotions serve as internal cues that move learners toward engagement and commitment to learning. In contrast, emotions such as fear and anxiety trigger avoidance and discomfort, undermining cognitive focus and memory retrieval, hindering deeper, more meaningful learning.

Negative emotions are not always detrimental. Negative emotions that create cognitive dissonance or disequilibrium are beneficial to the learning process. Cognitive disequilibrium happens when class members encounter something that does not fit their prior knowledge or beliefs. The incongruency creates a mental imbalance and pushes learners to make sense of the new information. They either fit the current information into what they already know (assimilation), or they change their thinking on the subject (accommodation). When assimilation and accommodation take place, the result is cognitive equilibrium. The learners consolidate understanding and build self-efficacy and confidence, which in turn enables deeper and more meaningful learning. Emotions play a significant role in motivating learners, either increasing or diminishing a desire to engage the content.

---

14. Sousa, *Rewired Bran*, 57.

Negative Emotions	Positive Emotions
• Discourage motivation	• Excite curiosity
• Decrease engagement	• Increase engagement
• Inhibit memory	• Trigger memories
• Trigger avoidance and discomfort	• Stimulate decision-making
• Undermine cognitive focus	• Focus creativity
• Disrupt appropriation	• Enhance appropriation

Aspects Related to Motivation

Although emotions play a crucial role in learning, motivation adds additional fuel to direct learners toward a meaningful pursuit of learning. Motivation is the drive that compels a person to act in a certain way; it provides direction and purpose, and influences decision-making. Learners come to class either ready to listen, engage, and learn or to ignore, disengage, or daydream. Effective motivation enhances classroom engagement and leads to higher levels of learning, skill acquisition, and positive behavioral change.

The two primary types of motivation are intrinsic motivation and extrinsic motivation. Extrinsic motivation relies on external rewards or outcomes, reflecting a "'What's the external value for me?' mentality . . . [that] emphasizes the values placed on the outcome" over the learning process itself.[15] In other words, class members' engagement in class depends upon the external rewards they receive after completing an activity. Educators sometimes refer to this type of motivation as a performance-oriented mindset. Learners perform to receive a good grade, a desired recognition, or to win a competition. These types of "rewards can deliver a short-term boost . . . but the effect wears off—and, worse, can reduce a person's longer-term motivation to continue the project."[16] Learners whose primary motivations are extrinsic will not prioritize pursuing deeper educational values such as mastery of content, skill development, or changes in behavior.

Although extrinsic motivators can sometimes reduce a learner's internal interest in learning, educators who use them intentionally and align them with personal goals can actually foster engagement and completion of more mentally demanding tasks. As learners become more competent, they might develop an internal motivation for deeper educational values. For example, students who take a Greek course begin with a focus on earning a

---

15. Graham, *Teaching Redemptively*, 152.
16. Pink, *Drive*, 8.

good grade or meeting a graduation requirement. As they gain confidence in translating the text, they discover that the language is deepening their understanding of Scripture, and their motivation begins to shift. They value the skill not only for better grades but as a tool to increase spiritual growth and interpretation of God's word. External motivators, when strategically integrated, can serve as a bridge to deeper intrinsic motivations.

Although extrinsic motivation can be useful, the caution in relying heavily on external motivation is that "over time, class members begin to see learning not as something they *want* to do but as a chore they *have* to do."[17] An external or performance mindset will eventually block engagement, curiosity, and long-term memory recall. In contrast, developing a more intrinsic motivation creates an internal desire to learn more. When learners begin to experience success, accompanied by positive feedback, affirmation, or encouragement, they begin to develop internal motivation and a growth mindset.

Intrinsic motivation occurs when learners' needs or goals align with their expectations, resulting in deeper engagement and retention. They ask, "What's the internal value for me?" Intrinsic motivation "emphasizes the value associated with an activity itself"[18] and reflects what educators call a growth mindset toward learning. There is a range of intrinsic motives, but "enjoyment-based intrinsic motivation, namely how creative a person feels when working on the project, is the strongest and most pervasive driver. The fun of mastering the challenge."[19] Mastery refers to a sense of improvement in knowledge, attitude, or skill. When learners recognize growth in a subject matter, the awareness of growth creates an internal sense of reward and initiates further motivation and learning. By giving learners clear goals, educators foster a growth or mastery mindset and help them view assignments and projects as opportunities for improvement. The goal is to learn or master the content, not to receive a reward.

In addition to mastery, autonomy and purpose are essential in capturing more intrinsic motivations. Autonomy means "acting with choice [and] has a powerful effect on individual performance and attitude. It promotes greater conceptual understanding, better grades, enhanced persistence at school and in sporting activities, higher productivity, less burnout, and greater levels of psychological well-being."[20] For example, allowing class members in a preaching course to choose their own text encourages them

---

17. Goodwin and Marzano, *New Classroom Instruction*, 13.
18. Graham, *Teaching Redemptively*, 152.
19. Lakhani and Wolf, "Hackers," 3, 12.
20. Pink, *Drive*, 90–91.

to connect the assignment with their interests, which can increase their internal motivation and engagement with the course.

Finally, intrinsically motivated learners benefit from identifying a personal purpose in mastering the content and recognizing learning goals as relevant to their lives or the lives of others. When learners feel a sense of purpose in class, they experience less anxiety and show greater engagement. For example, a class member's purpose in taking an Old Testament survey course might be to gain a deeper understanding of Scripture, not only to enrich personal study, but also to prepare sermons or Bible studies that transform others. Mastery, purpose, and autonomy all work together to strengthen intrinsic motivations and foster engagement in meaningful learning.

Extrinsic Motivation	Intrinsic Motivation
• Relies on external rewards • Can reduce desire to learn • Produces short-term results • Can lead to a performance mindset • Can serve as a bridge to deeper intrinsic motivation	• Relies on internal sense of reward • Fosters a desire to learn • Produces long-term results • Leads to a mastery mindset • Can develop out of appropriate extrinsic motivation

Aspects Related to Cultural and Social Dynamics

Each learner or educator brings to the classroom a unique set of beliefs, values, and behaviors that might differ from others in how they pursue their educational needs or goals. These differences contribute to a diverse educational experience, as personalities influence how learners engage their learning environment. When people of various ages and ethnicities come together, they not only participate in the institutional culture, but they also have the potential to influence and redefine it. For example, eye contact or physical proximity will differ among countries. Understanding and valuing learners' cultural background—particularly how they perceive authority, interpret information, respond to distinctive teaching styles, and participate in class—enables educators to adapt and design lessons either to address or to incorporate these differences. Furthermore, educators must recognize that they, too, have "been nurtured in a specific culture . . . [with] a specific cultural bias about teaching and learning."[21] For this reason, educators

---

21. Lingenfelter and Lingenfelter, *Teaching Cross-Culturally*, 32.

should give careful consideration in using idioms, movie references, sports analogies, or humor that might be unfamiliar or confusing to learners from other cultural backgrounds. Cultural bias can also affect how educators interpret learners' behavior.

Listening and asking questions is one of the most effective ways to learn about the differences and similarities between educational experiences and expectations. When educators take the time to know the learner, they reduce misunderstandings that could hinder meaningful participation. For example, in Asian cultures, silence often reflects respect for the teacher, whereas in Western classrooms, an educator might interpret a quiet student as disengaged or unprepared. Furthermore, in Asian cultures, low grades might carry a sense of social and familial shame. The Asian learning environment is typically structured, lecture-based, and teacher-centered. When learners from these backgrounds encounter a more interactive and autonomous teaching style, they might experience feelings of anxiety, inadequacy, or academic struggle as they adjust to unfamiliar expectations. If educators do not acknowledge or address these challenges, learners might feel misunderstood or anxious, and disengage from the course.

The challenge for educators is the tension between how to honor cultural differences while still ensuring academic success for all class members. Talking with class members is a starting point for understanding where they might feel uncertain, anxious, or confused. Additional strategies to help bridge cultural differences include incorporating culturally relevant examples when appropriate, varying instructional methods to accommodate different learning preferences, and clearly explaining how interactive approaches support understanding and engagement.

In addition to cultural background, social influences play a significant role in learners' motivation and engagement with both educators and classmates. In interactive learning environments, educators must be aware of the social dynamics shaping class members' willingness to participate. A lack of meaningful connection can hinder learning. Although social media increases the number of learners' interactions, it often reduces the depth and authenticity of those relationships. Both Scripture and neuroscience affirm that God wired humans for connection. From the beginning, God designed a world not only to satisfy humankind's physical needs but also their deepest longings for love and relationship.

Relationships are an essential part of human flourishing. In the classroom, creating a sense of classroom community that embraces cultural, social, and personal differences can enhance motivation and foster emotional safety. When learners feel secure, they are more likely to ask questions, seek help, and engage actively. As they develop positive connections and feel valued by educators and peers, their motivation and engagement tend to increase. Positive social experiences also strengthen cognitive functions such as memory, decision-making, and critical thinking.

Educators play a key role in modeling community. Welcoming members to class, offering positive feedback, meeting them before or after class, or providing opportunities for group discussion or collaborative projects, are some effective ways to foster connection and community. A strong sense of belonging can increase intrinsic motivations because learners believe that they have something to contribute.

Bridging Cultural and Social Differences
• Listen and ask respectful questions. • Incorporate culturally-relevant examples in instruction. • Vary instructional methods. • Explain how educational methods support learning. • Create a sense of classroom community.

Aspects Related to Receiving and Processing Information

Another factor to consider in knowing learners is the way in which they receive and process information. A common approach is to use the terms *learning styles* or *learning preferences* to describe "the concept that individuals differ in regard to what mode of instruction or study is most effective for them."[22] Although some educators argue that learners have preferred learning styles, other studies have questioned the effectiveness of classifying individuals by learning style.

Riechmann and Grasha first developed a scale of student learning styles in 1974.[23] Building on their foundation, Fleming focused on one aspect of the way in which individuals prefer to gather, organize, and think about information—instructional preferences. In 1987, he introduced the VARK model to set out a taxonomy of four instructional preferences that individuals use to take in information. He labeled those preferences as Visual, Aural, Read/Write, and Kinesthetic.[24] His model suggests that each prefer-

---

22. Pashler et al., "Learning Styles," 105.
23. Riechmann and Grasha, "Student Learning Style," 221–22.
24. Fleming, *VARK Strategies*, 1–2.

ence has distinctive characteristics and uses different strategies for taking in information. Other writers have proposed alternative labels for the same preferences, and with slight adjustments to the titles of the third and fourth categories, the following table provides a definition, characteristics, and strategies associated with each instructional preference:

Preference	Definition	Characteristics	Strategies
Visual	Learn by observing	Talk quickly / Prefer pictures	Use charts, graphs, images, videos
Aural	Learn by hearing	Listen carefully / Prefer spoken explanation	Use discussions, reports, lectures
Verbal	Learn by using words	Read and take notes well / Prefer written text	Use handouts, writing, quizzes
Physical	Learn by experiencing	Decide slowly / Prefer trial and error	Use experiments, case studies, role-plays

In 1983, Gardner suggested an alternate approach that identifies eight different types of intelligence that shape how students learn.[25] Without examining it in detail, his theory highlights differences in how students learn. The following table sets out the basics of Gardner's model:

Types of Intelligence		
Intelligence	How It Applies to the Learner	Practical Application
Linguistic	Connects through words, reading, writing, and speaking.	Use written assignments, discussions, journaling, and class presentations.
Logical-Mathematical	Enjoys problem-solving, patterns, and logical thinking.	Incorporate case studies, outlines, debates, and structured lessons.
Musical	Engages with rhythm, tone, and sound.	Integrate songs to reinforce content, combine music with reflection exercises.
Bodily-Kinesthetic	Retains more through movement, physical experience, and hands-on tasks.	Include role-play, object lessons, or rotating stations that involve movement.

---

25. Gardner, *Frames of Mind*, 173–76.

Spatial	Thinks in images or pictures; understands visual-spatial relationships.	Use diagrams, infographics, mind maps, slides, and visual aids during instruction.
Interpersonal	Understands and relates well to others.	Offer small groups, peer feedback, mentoring, or group projects.
Intrapersonal	Reflective and self-aware, values independent work and internal processing.	Assign reflection papers, silent journaling, goal setting, or formation tasks.
Naturalistic	Learns by observing nature and categorizing information.	Provide outdoor experiences or nature metaphors.

In summary, no two learners receive and process information in the same way. Although educators remain divided on the topic, using a multimodal approach to class and course design can improve motivation, engagement, and comprehension.

Aspects Related to Generational Traits

In addition to memory, emotion, motivation, culture, learning preferences, and kinds of intelligence, there is also a generational component that can influence how learners learn. Each generation brings distinct experiences shaped by culture, technology, communication styles, or other preferences, all of which can affect expectations in the classroom. At the same time, educators must remember that generational distinctions "are a *lens* through which to understand societal change, rather than a *label* with which to oversimplify differences between groups."[26] Each learner who enters the classroom will not exhibit every trait associated with his or her generation, but understanding these differences can offer helpful insights for knowing and engaging learners.

Presently, six generations are living, starting with the Silent Generation, and ending with the Polars or Generation Alpha. The majority of learners in higher education, however, belong to Generation X, Millennials, or Generation Z. In order to understand the learning needs of members of these generations, this section will provide a general overview of characteristics and influences as they relate to learning and engagement.

---

26. Dimock, "Where Millennials End," para. 18.

Six Living Generations			
Silents	1925–1945	**Millennials**	1980–1994
Boomers	1946–1964	**Generation Z**	1995–2012
Generation X	1965–1979	Polars/Generation Alpha	2013–2029

Generation X often receives less attention than other generations. As the smallest generational cohort, they frequently operate in the background while media spotlights the needs of Boomers, or the innovations of Millennials and Gen Z. Gen Xers grew up during a time of rising divorce rates and dual-income households. Many become known as "latchkey kids," who opened doors to empty houses. A lack of supervision gave them greater freedom to roam their neighborhoods and spend more time watching television. Television provided entertainment but also produced a consumer-driven mindset, encouraging extrinsic motivation for financial success, materialism, and personal significance. At school, educators reinforced a sense of individualistic motivation by emphasizing self-esteem and personal achievement.

Gen X was the last generation to grow up in a fully analog world and the first to encounter digital technology as young adults. This bridging of eras often cultivates resourcefulness, adaptability, and ease with technology that supports learning in both online and residential courses. Their cultural and educational experiences also contributed to a more individualist, self-reliant, and pragmatic approach to life and learning. Conversely, these attitudes might result in unrealistic expectations or resistance to collaborative learning models.

Gen X prefers to communicate via email, whereas Boomers favor phone calls or in-person conversations, and younger generations rely more on texting. In the classroom, they prefer the instructor to lecture instead of engaging in hands-on activities. Gen Xers are often skeptical when they engage authority. They might distrust institutions or question whether educators are acting in students' best interests. On the bright side, they are "less likely to question teaching methods . . . [and are] willing to challenge academic sources."[27]

What do these characteristics mean for educators? Gen X learners often value learning environments that emphasize clarity, concrete information, independence, and practical application. Their individualistic worldview, however, might hinder community building in the classroom, especially if

27. Figueiredo, "Millennial Learner," 5.

they mistrust peers, challenge authority, or resist group interaction. Their individualistic mindset "creates the idea that one person's view is just as good as another's despite differences in expertise."[28] Such an outlook might contribute to resistance to constructive feedback or reluctance to value the expertise of others. Recognizing these tendencies allows educators to affirm Gen X's strengths of self-reliance and confidence while also encouraging collaboration and mutual respect with instructors and peers.

Traits of Generation X	
• Motivated by financial success and personal significance. • Resourceful and adaptable in using technology. • Individualistic, self-reliant, confident, and pragmatic. • Prefer to communicate by email.	• Prefer lecture to hands-on activity. • Resistant to collaboration and feedback. • Skeptical toward authority. • Value clarity, concreteness, and practical application.

Millennials grew up in a culture of individualism and self-focus with phrases such as "believe in yourself" and "anything is possible." Many grew up with "helicopter parents" who hovered over and protected nearly every aspect of their lives, often intervening in school, relationships, and extracurricular activities. In school settings, educators often rewarded learners equally to avoid damaging their self-esteem. Such practices tended to reduce competition while fostering a sense of entitlement. When educators affirmed identity rather than assessing mastery, learners received higher grades but spent less time on homework than previous generations.

Younger millennials might still live alone or with their parents. They popularized the term *adulting* to describe "boring but necessary grown-up activities such as working, paying bills, and doing laundry"[29] that previous generations considered a normal part of life. They could receive "merit badges" for completing some of these adult activities. Educators and parents emphasized self-esteem rather than practical life skills. Some critics, however, describe their self-esteem as empty because it "concludes that feeling good about yourself is so important that your actions or actual gifts don't matter."[30] Educators were validating learners on the basis of who they were rather than on what they learned. Millennials, therefore, have elevated expectations for themselves and have more optimism and confidence than

28. Twenge, *Generations*, 203.
29. Twenge, *Generations*, 233.
30. Twenge, *Generations*, 243.

any other generation. The problem with this mindset is that some of them might lack motivation, resist critical feedback, or expect high grades simply for attending class.[31] These narcissistic tendencies, however, tend to decline in older millennials.[32]

Younger Millennials grew up immersed in technology. They prefer texting over phone calls and expect fast-paced, technology-savvy environments. Growing up in the digital age shaped their expectations. As a result, they often have shorter attention spans, become bored easily, expect quick feedback, prefer multimedia learning experiences, and value flexibility in teaching methods.

In addition to these learning preferences, Millennials tend to spend less time socializing than previous generations did. They engage more effectively and learn more when they participate in hands-on activities, simulations, team-based presentations, and real-world case scenarios rather than listening to lectures. Despite these strengths, they are also more likely to bring "hedonism, narcissism, and [a] cavalier work ethic" to the classroom, often expecting rewards and recognition for a job well done.[33]

Millennials also bring values of purpose and authenticity to the classroom, preferring course content to connect with real-life issues. They value work that has personal meaning or can benefit others. Some researchers, however, perceive this attitude as coming from a consumer-driven mindset that causes the group to "see themselves as customers in a business transaction, seeking direct benefit and application from education as the product."[34] Ultimately, they want to see the relevance to the real world and how education will benefit them when they graduate. They also value educators who provide clear goals, regular feedback, and recognition for a job well done.

To foster learning and engagement among Millennials, educators should balance challenges with encouragement, build a sense of community, limit reliance on lectures, and incorporate active learning strategies. Connecting lessons to real-world problems helps clarify the relevance of the content. Millennials expect fast, constructive feedback and recognition for their efforts, both of which increase motivation to learn. They respond well to opportunities for leadership and personal growth. Educators who bring energy and passion for the subject matter, along with frequent praise, often see an increase in engagement and enthusiasm to learn. Some millennials, however, might struggle with criticism as a result of overconfidence and a

31. Goyal and Gupta, "Millennials in Higher Education," 3–4.
32. Twenge, *Generations*, 253–54.
33. Alexander and Sysko, "I'm Gen Y," 127.
34. Figueiredo, "Millennial Learner," 7.

sense of entitlement. The overall goal is to create a welcoming, collaborative community atmosphere while still upholding academic rigor.

Traits of Millennials	
• Possess elevated levels of expectation, optimism, and confidence. • Expect fast-paced technological environments. • Lack motivation and have short attention spans. • Might resist criticism or undervalue expertise.	• Prefer to communicate by texting. • Prefer collaboration and hands-on activity to lecture. • Value purpose, authenticity, and real-world application. • Value clear goals, regular encouragement, and prompt feedback.

Generation Z will require educators to make further adjustments to meet their needs as they enter the classroom.[35] Perhaps the most notable characteristic of Gen Z is digital distraction; they are "unable to concentrate for more than a few seconds on any one thing."[36] As a result, their "brains are wired differently than those [of] past [generations]."[37] Early and frequent use of digital technology, especially smartphones, made a measurable impact on Gen Z's behavior, cognitive development, and social skills. As a result, they exhibit the following traits:

1. Elevated levels of anxiety.
2. Decrease in attention spans.
3. Decline in cognitive efficiency.
4. Decline in long-term memory.
5. Diminished ability to reflect deeply and engage in critical thinking skills.
6. Fewer hours spent reading books.
7. Reduced ability to delay gratification.
8. Preference for working alone rather than in groups.
9. Less sleep and more screen-induced fatigue.
10. Hesitancy to speak up or ask questions in class.

---

35. Portions of this section are adapted from Rabon, "Teaching Strategies."
36. Zarra, *Entitled Generation*, xii.
37. Zarra, *Entitled Generation*, 48.

In contrast to Gen X, who grew up talking face-to-face, playing outdoors, or going to a physical library, Gen Z tends to interact through texting, posting, and video gaming. Disconnection with the physical world can lead to negative mental, emotional, physical, and spiritual consequences. A constant flood of information contributes to an increase in loneliness, stress, isolation, and anxiety, which often spills over into their academic performance. Faced with cognitive overload, many Gen Zers opt for brief videos or summaries over more rigorous reading and research. Some resort to plagiarism as a way to cope with academic pressure. These learners are "wired for speed . . . and expect to learn things quickly, otherwise they are bored, give up, and move on."[38] Unfortunately, technology creates the illusion that answers are only a click away. Their rapid approach to learning hinders Gen Z's skills to problem-solve, think critically, analyze, and synthesize. Many rely on external tools (e.g., AI, Grammarly, Google) rather than processing information internally.

Gen Zers also believe that they can multitask effectively. The problem with multitasking is that individuals "switch back and forth between tasks so frequently that [they] think [they] are doing more than one thing at once, but [they] rarely are . . . you can't type a text into your smartphone and read a schoolbook at the same time."[39] Educators who permit learners to use smartphones in class find that those class members score lower on exam questions, highlighting the long-term academic problems of divided attention.

Online reading habits further reinforce shallow processing. Gen Zers tend to skim one or two pages before clicking to another site. This skimming activity weakens the "ability to interpret text, to make the rich mental connections that form when [people] read deeply and without distraction."[40] The internet is rewiring the brain to operate at high-speed frequencies, which can damage attention, concentration, and deep thinking.

Despite these challenges, Gen Z brings unique strengths to the classroom. They are known to be curious, entrepreneurial, career-driven, loyal, justice-oriented, and concerned for others. They tend to "work hard and [are] less likely to vociferously question their grades," than Millennials.[41] Many pursue degrees not simply for learning, but for the promise of financial security. Although a more pragmatic mindset can hinder an intrinsic love of learning, it reflects a more goal-oriented approach.

38. Zarra, *Entitled Generation*, 57–58, 66.
39. Kutscher and Rosin, "Your Child with ADHD," 24.
40. Carr, "Is Google Making Us Stupid?," 58.
41. Twenge, *iGen*, 307.

Gen Zers prefer "hands-on experiences that allow them to situate themselves in the middle of the learning rather than on the periphery as an observer."[42] More than previous generations, they need modeling, structured guidance, and opportunities for reflection. Instructors who incorporate these classroom adjustments help create the neural pathways necessary for deeper thinking, processing, and learning.

They also prefer "learning independently and at their own pace."[43] Their hesitancy to participate in class often stems from a desire to avoid judgment or failure. Many of them struggle with overload anxiety or FOMO (fear of missing out), which makes clear structure and limited choices essential for reducing stress and improving academic performance. Helpful strategies to use with Gen Z learners include

1. scaffolding large project deadlines into smaller milestones;
2. providing clear instructions and expectations (e.g., page length, formatting);
3. furnishing past project examples, rubrics, checklists, and video tips on how to complete the assignment; and
4. offering assignment options (i.e., a five-page paper, a ten-minute video, or a fifteen-minute presentation) to boost motivation and engagement.

Educators can also tap into Gen Z's relational motivations to increase engagement. Seemiller and Grace write, "70 percent of Generation Z students are motivated by not wanting to let others down."[44] Group projects, team presentations, and other activities that highlight mutual responsibility reinforce a more we-centric attitude.

Traits of Generation Z	
• Possess elevated levels of loneliness, anxiety, stress, and isolation. • Are curious, entrepreneurial, career-driven, and concerned for others. • Prefer texting, posting, and video gaming. • Have short attention spans. • Tend to skim and multitask.	• Are hesitant to participate in class. • Prefer hands-on experiences. • Prefer working independently and at their own pace. • Rely on external tools instead of internal processing. • Need modeling, structure, and opportunities for reflection.

42. Seemiller and Grace, *Generation Z Learns*, 67.
43. Seemiller and Grace, *Generation Z Goes to College*, 178.
44. Seemiller and Grace, *Generation Z Goes to College*, 15.

Although understanding generational traits provides helpful insight, it is only one aspect of the learner. Each class member brings a unique blend of experiences, emotional needs, motivations, and cultural and social backgrounds to the classroom. In order to know their learners, educators must cultivate personal connections.

Practical Strategies for Getting to Know the Learner

Educators can move from a broader understanding of their learners to a more personal connection through intentional observation, assessment, and interaction with them. One effective strategy is to collect information at three key stages—before, during, and after class—so that they better understand students' motivations, backgrounds, and learning preferences.

Gather initial insights before the class begins. A brief pre-course survey allows educators to gather important insights about learners' expectations, learning preferences, and readiness for the course. Here are several possible survey questions:

1. What do you hope to gain personally from the course?
2. What learning environment makes you feel anxious, comfortable, or curious?
3. What are your preferred learning styles?
4. What motivates you to learn?
5. What are your strengths or weaknesses as a learner?
6. What types of teaching methods help you engage more effectively (e.g., lecture, discussions, hands-on activities)?
7. What helps you stay engaged?
8. What might prevent you from learning or completing assignments?
9. What is your preferred method of study?
10. What kind of feedback is helpful to you?

These questions not only help assess motivation and preferences; they also demonstrate a commitment to listening and fostering a collaborative learning environment. The survey equips educators to tailor their teaching and activities for more meaningful learning and engagement.

Connect through observation and interaction during class. Instructors can continue learning about class members through structured activities and informal interactions. A simple step is to learn and use learners' names during class. Calling them by name communicates respect and helps cultivate a sense of community in the classroom. Educators can also distribute a survey on the first day of class to connect class members with their names, assess prior knowledge, spark curiosity, and gather other important information that can guide the selection of teaching strategies to align them more closely with learners' needs and goals. Here is a brief sample survey that class members might complete at the beginning of an undergraduate course on Romans; it would provide information on class members' educational backgrounds and interests as they begin the course:

Getting to Know You
What is your name?
What is your email address?
What are your major and your career goal?
What is your class? (Circle one.) 　　　Freshman　　Sophomore　　Junior　　Senior
Which of the following courses have you taken? (Circle all that apply.) 　　　OT Survey　　NT Survey　　Hermeneutics　　Christian Theology
Which of the course objectives seems most useful to you? (Check one.) ☐ Assess evidence related to the Introductory Questions for Romans. ☐ Create a graphic overview of the content, argument, and themes of Romans. ☐ Interpret selected passages in Romans using sound hermeneutical principles. ☐ Discuss how biblical teachings from Romans apply to your own life. ☐ Outline in detail the argument of Romans. ☐ Develop a plan for leading others through the study of Romans.
What is something that you hope to learn in this course?
What do you already know about the book of Romans?

Educators can also supplement academic content with interactive exercises that foster community and connection. One simple activity is to have class members line up facing each other as the educator calls out questions such as, "What is your favorite movie?" or "How do you spend your free time?" After a one-minute exchange, learners rotate to face new partners and continue the activity until everyone has a chance to meet one another. These brief conversations can ease anxiety, encourage interaction, and help class members discover shared interests.

In addition to fostering personal connections, educators must also consider deeper elements of learner identity. Cultural understanding is another essential component of knowing the learner. Instructors can invite class members to share aspects of their cultural background through guided questions or discussion prompts. These types of dialogue will build awareness and appreciation of differences, as well as foster a respectful learning environment. Educators can also gain valuable insight by observing nonverbal cues, such as facial expressions, tone of voice, and body language, which often reveal levels of engagement, confusion, boredom, anxiety, or enthusiasm for the subject matter. Responding to these cues in real time allows for timely instructional adjustments and reinforces learner-centered teaching.

Continue building rapport after class. Educators can continue building rapport through informal conversations, prayer, shared meals, or open office hours. These times provide insight into class members' personal and academic needs, wins, or challenges, and increase the educator's knowledge of how to offer meaningful support. Over time, all of these practices can contribute to better educator-learner and peer relationships. In turn, those relationships contribute to a learning environment that is academically and personally beneficial to everyone.

Conclusion

Educators can never fully know all of the factors that influence learners during their academic journeys. Nevertheless, there is immense value in recognizing that "every student is unique and brings contributions that no one else can make."[45] By approaching learning with an attitude of respect for class members and a desire to know them, educators strengthen their ability to meet learners' academic needs. The excitement of teaching comes from the truth that no two classes will ever be the same, because no two learners are ever the same.

---

45. Bain, *Best College Teachers*, 72.

Food for Thought
What assumptions about learners do you need to overcome that would help increase engagement and meaningful learning?
What practices could you incorporate to build a deeper sense of community in the classroom?
What are the benefits of respecting other cultures and generational differences in regard to your course structure and content?
What is one course that you teach in which you could incorporate a pre-class or in-class questionnaire in order to know class members in greater depth?

3

Define the Learning: The Importance of a Well-Defined Course

Chapter Preview
A learning-centered approach to course design considers different learning preferences, begins with course and unit outcomes, addresses three domains of learning, and aims to include three levels of learning.
Essential questions to answer in defining a learning-centered course are: (1) Who are the learners? (2) What are the goals? (3) What is the evidence? (4) What is the plan?
The key to designing a course is defining the course. The course definition becomes the basis for designing a well-structured course syllabus.

THE GOAL IS LEARNING, and meaningful learning begins with course design. One common approach to course design focuses on content coverage. In other words, the course design process runs something like this:

1. Determine the scope of the course content. The overall curriculum of which the course is a part often sets the scope.
2. Decide on the textbook(s). The textbook(s) usually relate to the content area(s) that fall within the scope of the course.

3. Divide the content into segments. The segments usually relate to the number of weeks and/or class sessions in the term during which the course will run.
4. Design activities and assignments that class members will complete. The activities and assignments usually relate to specific content.
5. Develop a schedule that sets out when class members will work on the content segments and assignments.
6. Draft a syllabus that includes outcomes for the course and the means of assessing student work during the course.

Such an approach moves from instruction to outcomes, gives priority to content coverage rather than to student learning, and focuses on assessing the degree to which learners acquire information related to the topic they are studying. It tends to be teaching-centered rather than learning-centered.

Two Learning-Centered Approaches

Toward the end of the last century, Wiggins and McTighe proposed an alternate approach that they called "backward design." The approach is "backward" because it moves from outcomes to instruction rather than moving from instruction to outcomes as in the approach outlined above. They proposed the following three-step design process:

1. Identify desired results.
2. Determine acceptable evidence.
3. Plan learning experiences and instruction.[1]

Five years later, Fink proposed an expanded version of backward design that he introduced as "integrated design." Fink's approach included twelve steps:

1. Consider situational factors.
2. Identify learning goals.
3. Formulate feedback and assessment procedures.
4. Select teaching and learning activities.
5. Integrate key components.
6. Create a thematic structure.

---

1. Wiggins and McTighe, *Understanding by Design*, 17.

7. Select a teaching strategy.
8. Create an overall scheme of learning activities.
9. Develop the grading system.
10. Debug possible problems.
11. Write the syllabus.
12. Plan an evaluation.[2]

In Fink's approach, the three steps of backward design became the second, third, and fourth steps of a considerably more detailed model. Both models move from outcomes to instruction, give priority to student learning rather than to content coverage, and focus on assessing the degree to which learners achieve outcomes related to the topic they are studying. Together these alternative approaches suggest four essential questions that should inform a learning-centered approach to course design: (1) Who are the learners? (2) What are the goals? (3) What is the evidence? (4) What is the plan?

Question #1: Who Are the Learners?

Fink listed "consider situational factors" as the first step in his model. There are, perhaps, no more significant situational factors than the worldviews, values, attitudes, and instructional preferences of the learners who will take the course. For that reason, the first question in Vella's seven-step dialogue-learning lesson plan design process is "Who?"[3] Although Vella focuses on the identity and number of participants and leaders, it is also important to consider their attitudes, their expectations, and their instructional preferences.

Chapter 2 has already discussed aspects related to learners' memories, emotions, motivations, cultural and social dynamics, generational distinctives, and how they receive and process information. Reflection on those aspects will help paint a general portrait of the individuals who will be part of the course. Using a pre-course or a first-day-of-class survey can help sharpen the focus of the portrait. See chapter 2 for an example.

---

2. Fink, *Significant Learning Experiences*, 74–75.
3. Vella, *On Teaching and Learning*, 32.

Question #2: What Are the Goals?

Both backward design and integrated design emphasize the importance of goals and their use as the starting point for learning-centered course design. Ideally, course goals will relate upward to program goals and downward to unit goals, lesson goals, and assignment goals.

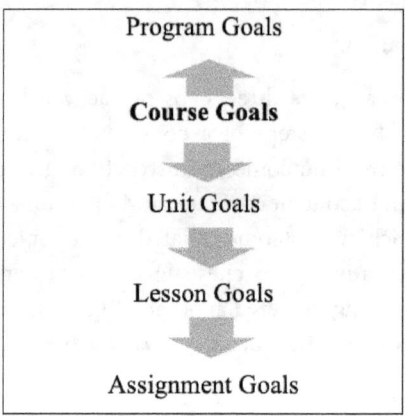

Many course goals tend to be ability-based. That is, they describe what learners should be able to do after they have completed the course as a function of the teaching in the course. For example, a list of objectives in a course syllabus might look like this:

Upon completion of this course, class members will be able to

1. list the author, date, provenance, destination, purpose, genre, and literary features of Paul's Letter to the Romans;

2. summarize the content and argument of Romans, including key issues and themes described in the letter; and

3. explain the significance of Paul's writings for the development of early Christian thought.

Vella takes a different approach and advocates the use of "achievement-based objectives" (ABOs) that describe what learners will have done as the result of engaging the knowledge and skills that are part of the course.[4] Goals stated as ABOs for the same course might look like this:

Upon completion of this course, class members will have

1. listed the author, date, provenance, destination, purpose, genre, and literary features of Paul's Letter to the Romans;

---

4. Vella, *On Teaching and Learning*, 42.

2. summarized the content and argument of Romans, including key issues and themes described in the letter; and

3. explained the significance of Paul's writings for the development of early Christian thought.

Wiggins and McTighe view true understanding as the ability to transfer knowledge and skills to new settings. They prefer framing goals in terms of "transfer tasks."[5] Goals for the Romans course that aim to develop skills learners can apply to other books of the Bible might look like this:

Upon completion of this course, class members will have learned how to

1. list the evidence related to the introductory questions of a biblical book;

2. summarize key issues and themes in a biblical book; and

3. explain the significance of a biblical book for Christian thought as a whole.

In the preceding examples, however, all of the sets of course goals have two elements in common. First, they all aim for relatively lower levels of learning, and second, they all fall into the cognitive domain of learning. Well-designed learning-centered courses include goals at multiple levels and in three domains. It is essential, therefore to understand and address different domains and levels of learning.

In 1956, Bloom first edited a handbook that presented a taxonomy of learning objectives for the cognitive domain and included six levels (lowest to highest): *knowledge, comprehension, application, analysis, synthesis, evaluation.*[6] Krathwohl, Bloom, and Masia subsequently published a taxonomy for the affective domain with five levels (lowest to highest): *receiving, responding, valuing, organizing, characterizing.*[7] Armstrong followed with three psychomotor variables: *frequency, energy, duration.*[8] The German Education Council also developed a four-category taxonomy of learned competencies (lowest to highest): *reproduce, reorganize, transfer, problem-solve.*[9] A team of educators subsequently divided the cognitive domain into knowledge and process dimensions and created a revised two-dimensional

---

5. Wiggins and McTighe, *Understanding by Design*, 78.
6. Bloom, *Cognitive Domain*, 18.
7. Krathwohl et al., *Affective Domain*, 35.
8. Armstrong, *Behavioral Objectives*, 22.
9. Cited in Weichhart, "S-BPM Education," 183.

taxonomy table in 2014.[10] Although Bloom's taxonomy for the cognitive domain is the best-known and the most widely used, a learning-centered approach to course design addresses all three domains. The model proposed in this book uses the categories of content, character, and competence rather than cognitive, affective, and behavioral.

Advocating for a model of Bible teaching that aims for transformation, Richards proposed three levels of learning that included four elements:[11]

Element	Level 1	Level 2	Level 3
Focus	Information	General Relevance	Personal Relevance
Objective	Understanding	Implications	Responses
Involvement	Ideas	Past Experiences	Present Experiences
Relationship	Superficial	Reserved	Deep

Adapting Richards's model slightly and adding the three domains of learning suggests a three-level multitiered approach to balanced course design:

Element	Level 1	Level 2	Level 3
Focus	Information	Appropriation	Transformation
Objective	Ideas	Implications	Responses
Involvement	Listening	Reflecting	Engaging
Content	Comprehend	Analyze	Create
Character	Receive	Respond	Value
Competence	Reproduce	Reorganize	Innovate

Balanced, learning-centered courses, units, and lessons will seek to include all three levels and will include goals that address all three domains. The lesson plan model in chapter 6 seems particularly well-suited to balance different levels of goals in all three domains. Returning to the Romans

---

10. Anderson and Krathwohl, *Taxonomy for Learning*, 27–31. See also 268 for a helpful summary chart.

11. Richards, *You and Adults*, 56.

course above, a more well-rounded set of course goals (stated as ABOs) might be:

By the end of this course, class members will have

1. created a graphic overview that summarizes the content, argument, and themes of Romans (Level 1, Content);

2. reported on how they have applied biblical teachings from Romans to daily Christian living (Level 2, Character); and

3. completed four exegetical assignments that interpret selected passages in Romans using sound hermeneutical principles (Level 3, Competence).

Verbs are the key to writing program, course, unit, and lesson goals, and it is important to choose verbs that address the learning domains and levels thoughtfully. A variety of internet sites provide lists of verbs for each domain and level, and Vella includes a list of "tough verbs for learning tasks."[12] The following table is suggestive rather than exhaustive:

	Level 1	Level 2	Level 3
Content	Comprehend Define Describe Identify Interpret List Outline Paraphrase Recognize Summarize Understand	Analyze Assess Categorize Critique Distinguish Evaluate Illustrate Prioritize Relate Report Review	Create Compile Compose Design Develop Devise Formulate Integrate Organize Plan Synthesize

---

12. Vella, *On Teaching and Learning*, 221.

Character	Receive Accept Ask Choose Describe Follow Identify Locate Name Read Recognize	Respond Answer Complete Discuss Examine Label Present Recite Report Select Write	Value Adopt Advocate Affirm Commit Initiate Justify Participate Promote Recommend Support
Competence	Reproduce Collect Compile Copy Follow Outline Record Repeat Review Summarize Trace	Reorganize Adapt Adjust Arrange Change Consolidate Distribute Group Modify Revise Systematize	Innovate Assemble Combine Compose Construct Create Design Develop Devise Establish Plan

Regardless of the verbs used, of course, the goal of writing goals is to clarify the learning that the course will seek to facilitate. Having identified the goals, the next step in learning-centered course design is determining how to assess the extent to which learners achieve those goals. In order to ensure that the assessment is valid, it is essential to establish acceptable evidence and appropriate means of assessment.

Question #3: What Is the Evidence?

After considering the worldviews, values, attitudes, and instructional preferences of the learners who will take the course and identifying the desired goals for a course, a learning-centered approach to course design establishes acceptable evidence for assessing whether learners achieve those goals. Determining what constitutes acceptable evidence involves answering two further questions: What evidence best demonstrates whether class members achieve each goal, and what means of assessment best measures whether class members achieve that goal? The evidence that best demonstrates whether learners achieve a given goal relates to the level of learning the goal addresses. The following table provides a basic framework for assessing achievement at each of the three levels of learning:

Level 1	Level 2	Level 3
Learners can **explain** the concept, attitude, or skill in their own words.	Learners can **evaluate** the concept, attitude, or skill using critical thinking.	Learners can **employ** the concept, attitude, or skill in new situations.

In other words, what deliverable(s) will learners produce to demonstrate that they can explain, evaluate, or employ the new concept, attitude, or skill that the goal emphasizes? Stating a goal as an ABO is particularly helpful, since that approach either implicitly or explicitly incorporates the deliverable into the goal itself. The last set of goals for the Romans course illustrates this approach:

By the end of this course, class members will have

1. created a graphic overview that *summarizes* the content, argument, and themes of Romans;
2. reported on how they have *applied* biblical teachings from Romans to daily Christian living; and
3. completed four exegetical assignments that *interpret* selected passages in Romans using sound hermeneutical principles.

The deliverable for the first goal will be an outline, table, chart, or picture. The deliverable for the second goal will be either a verbal or written report, perhaps in the form of a daily or weekly journal. The deliverable for the third goal will record the results of four exegetical assignments.

It is necessary, of course, to go beyond the basic framework to establish more specific criteria to assess achievement as well as levels of achievement related to each criterion. Chapter 5 will explore the details of assessment in greater detail, including delineating clear assessment criteria, setting appropriate scale levels, and writing precise performance descriptions for multidimensional rubrics that provide feedback and evaluate evidence of learning at assignment, unit, course, and program levels. Creating rubrics for assessment is an essential step between defining a course (this chapter) and designing the syllabus for a course (chapter 4). Once the evidence for assessment is in place, it becomes possible to select the means of assessment that will comprise the assignments for the course.

The means of assessment that best measures whether students achieve a given goal also relates to the level of learning the goal addresses. Wiggins and McTighe note a continuum of assessment means that include (from lowest to highest): *questions, observations, dialogues, quizzes/tests, academic prompts,* and *performance tasks.* Questions, observations, and dialogues most commonly occur throughout the learning process, are informal, and do not usually factor into grading. Quizzes and tests are familiar means of assessment. They define an academic prompt as an "open-ended question that requires students to think critically and prepare a specific academic response" and a performance task as a "complex challenge that mirrors issues and problems" related to the learning goal.[13] The latter three means of assessment correlate generally to the three levels of learning set out in the preceding section and suggest the kinds of the assignments that students might complete as they pursue goals at each level:

Level 1	Level 2	Level 3
Quizzes/Tests	Academic Prompts	Performance Tasks

Establishing acceptable evidence, therefore, leads directly to identifying assignments that might be part of a course. Before incorporating assignments into a course syllabus, however, it is necessary to create a course definition that sets out clearly and concisely the elements of the course that will remain constant regardless of the modality or duration of the course. The next section focuses on the task of defining a course as the basis for designing the syllabus.

Question #4: What Is the Plan?

The idea of defining a course might be a new one for many educators, especially if they have been teaching for a number of years. Why not just start with the syllabus? Why add another task to what is most likely an already busy schedule of course preparation and teaching? The answer to those questions, as discussed above, is that a learning-centered approach to course design moves from goals to instruction, gives priority to learning, and focuses on assessing the degree to which learners achieve outcomes related to the topic that they are studying. The process of defining a course, therefore, begins by describing the typical learner and identifying the goals that they should achieve by the end of the course. There are nine steps in the process of defining a course:

13. Wiggins and McTighe, *Understanding by Design,* 152.

1. Describe typical learners.
2. Draft a course description.
3. Establish course goals.
4. Determine the units.
5. Allocate goals to units.
6. Determine assignments that will measure learning.
7. Align assignments with unit outcomes.
8. Select readings and resources.
9. Allocate workload and grade weighting.

The following template serves as a guide through the process:

Course Definition Template		
Typical Learners		
Typical learners will be . . .		
Course Description		
In this course, you will . . .		
Course Goals		
By the end of this course, you will have	Domain	Level
1.		
2.		
3.		
4.		
5.		
Unit #1—		
Goals: By the end of this unit, you will have	Assignments	
1a		
1b		

1c	
Unit #2—	
Goals: By the end of this unit, you will have	Assignments
2a	
2b	
2c	
Unit #3—	
Goals: By the end of this unit, you will have	Assignments
3a	
3b	
3c	
Unit #4—	
Goals: By the end of this unit, you will have	Assignments
4a	
4b	
4c	
Unit #5—	
Goals: By the end of this unit, you will have	Assignments
5a	
5b	
5c	

Readings and Resources

You will need the following readings and resources for the course:

Assignments, Workload, and Grade Weighting

	hours		%
	hours		%
	hours		%
	hours		%
	hours		%

		hours	%
	Total	135 hours	100%

The first step is to *describe typical learners* who will participate in the course. Although the description will necessarily be preliminary, it should include as much information as you can project about the learners who will be in the course. What is their age range? Are they working while they are studying? What is their educational level? What background knowledge and experience do they bring to the specific topic of the course? How does the course fit into their educational and professional goals? Of which generation are they part? What are their learning preferences? It should be possible to summarize the information concisely in one paragraph. Here is an example for a seminary-level biblical studies course on Paul's Letter to the Romans:

Typical Learners
Typical learners will be at least twenty-five years old. Two-thirds are married, working full time, and studying part time. They have completed a previous baccalaureate degree, but only one in three has completed a previous degree in biblical-theological studies. Their level of biblical-theological knowledge varies widely as does the anticipated next step in their professional lives. All have some work and/or ministry experience. As members of Generation Z, they tend to prefer learning-centered strategies, such as case studies, gamification, or other experiential activities over passive activities such as lectures.

The second step is to *draft a course description*. In many instances, the course description will already be written and included in an academic catalog. In those situations, the easy solution is to incorporate the catalog description directly into the template. If it is necessary to write a description for a brand-new course, shorter is usually better than longer, and second person is usually better than third person. Chapter 4 will address how to write engaging copy for a syllabus, including the course description. Here is a course description for that same biblical studies course on Romans:

Course Description
In this course, you will focus on the New Testament's most organized, thorough exposition of Christian faith and its implications for Christian living. You will give special attention to the personal application of the message and will apply principles of biblical interpretation to the study of this letter.

The third step is to *establish course goals*. This step is the heart of a learning-centered course definition, since the goals lay the foundation on which the other elements of the course rest. Three to six goals is a manageable number for a course, and they should address different domains and levels of learning. Writing all course and unit goals as ABOs is a good practice to adopt and helps focus on achievements within the course rather than on aspirations after the course.

Course Goals		
By the end of this course, you will have	Domain	Level
1. Assessed evidence related to the Introductory Questions for Romans.	Content	2
2. Created a graphic overview of the content, argument, and themes of Romans.	Competence	3
3. Interpreted selected passages in Romans using sound hermeneutical principles.	Competence	3
4. Discussed how biblical teachings from Romans apply to your own life.	Character	2
5. Outlined in detail the argument of Romans.	Content	1
6. Developed a plan for leading others through a study of Romans.	Competence	3

The fourth step is to *determine the units*. After identifying the key ideas, implications, and responses for the course as a whole, organizing those elements into a logical sequence for students to follow defines the structure for the course. Fink recommends four to seven segments (units) that build upon one another and increase in complexity.[14] A basic structure that incorporates the three levels of learning would be the following:

```
                    | Unit 3 (Level 3 Learning) |
          | Unit 2 (Level 2 Learning) |
| Unit 1 (Level 1 Learning) |
```

In the example of the biblical studies course in Romans, the four major sections of the letter suggest a total of six units: one unit to introduce the

---

14. Fink, *Significant Learning Experiences*, 143. See also 62 for a chart that depicts how a learning-centered approach moves learners through multiple levels of learning.

study, four units to focus on the major sections of the letter, and one unit to conclude the study.

1	Grasping the Big Picture of Romans	
2	Interpreting and Applying Romans 1–4	The Revelation of God's Righteousness
3	Interpreting and Applying Romans 5–8	The Demonstration of God's Power
4	Interpreting and Applying Romans 9–11	The Fulfillment of God's Plan
5	Interpreting and Applying Romans 12–16	The Transformation of God's People
6	Capturing and Communicating the Message of Romans	

The fifth step is to *allocate goals to units*. The allocation can take either of two possible approaches. One approach is to divide the course goals among the units. Another approach is to establish sub-goals for each unit that "unpack" one or more course goals. The first approach is simpler; the second allows for greater detail. Sometimes, the same goal might appear in more than one unit. The following partial example takes the simpler approach of using the course goals as unit goals:

Unit #1—Grasping the Big Picture of Romans	
Goals: By the end of this unit, you will have	
1a Assessed evidence related to the Introductory Questions for Romans.	
1b Created a graphic overview of the content, argument, and themes of Romans.	
Unit #2—Interpreting and Applying Romans 1–4 **The Revelation of God's Righteousness**	
Goals: By the end of this unit, you will have	
2a Discussed how biblical teachings from Romans apply to your own life.	
2b Interpreted selected passages in Romans using sound hermeneutical principles.	

The sixth step is to *determine assignments that will measure learning*. What evidence best demonstrates whether students achieve each goal, and what means of assessment best measures whether students achieve that goal? Those questions return to the discussion above of the three levels of learning as well as the types of assignments.

Level 1	Level 2	Level 3
Learners can *explain* the concept, attitude, or skill in their own words.	Learners can *evaluate* the concept, attitude, or skill using critical thinking.	Learners can *employ* the concept, attitude, or skill in new situations.
Assessed by *quizzes/tests*.	Assessed by *academic prompts*.	Assessed by *performance tasks*.

The specific deliverables that provide the best means of measuring learning will vary with the particular course and discipline. It is best, however, to correlate the assignment with the domain and level of learning for each goal. In the example of the Romans course, the proposed assignments consist of a final exam, weekly academic prompts, and a series of performance tasks.

Goal	Domain	Level	Assignment
Assess evidence related to Introductory Questions.	Content	2	Learning Task (academic prompt)
Create a graphic overview of the content, argument, and themes.	Competence	3	Synthetic Study (performance task)
Interpret selected passages using sound hermeneutical principles.	Competence	3	Exegetical Practice (performance task)
Discuss how biblical teachings apply to life.	Character	2	Learning Task (academic prompt)
Outline in detail the argument.	Content	1	Final Exam (exam)
Develop a plan for leading others through a study.	Competence	3	Practical Project (performance task)

The seventh step is to *align assignments with unit goals*. Aligning one or more assignments with each unit goal keeps the focus on goals. It also tightens the internal coherence of the course and avoids the pitfall of assigning work that might be fun and/or interesting but that does not contribute to students learning the big ideas that should be the focus of the course.

Unit #1—Grasping the Big Picture of Romans	
Goals: By the end of this unit, you will have	Assignments
1a Assessed evidence related to the Introductory Questions for Romans.	Learning tasks on Romans 1:1–17 and 15:14—16:27
1b Created a graphic overview of the content, argument, and themes of Romans.	Synthetic study
Unit #2—Interpreting and Applying Romans 1-4 The Revelation of God's Righteousness	
Goals: By the end of this unit, you will have	Assignments
2a Discussed how biblical teachings from Romans apply to your own life.	Learning tasks on Romans 1:1—4:25
2b Interpreted selected passages in Romans using sound hermeneutical principles.	Exegetical practice on Romans 3:21–26

The eighth step is to *select readings and resources*. In content-centered course design, selecting textbooks is often one of the first steps. In learning-centered course design, selecting textbooks is always one of the last steps. The question is not "What books do the best job of covering the course content?" Instead, the question is "What books do the best job of helping students achieve the course goals?" As will become clear in the next step, the number of pages of reading for a course has a direct impact on the allocation of student workload hours. A reasonable top limit for moderately-to-highly-complex reading is 600–750 total pages.

Readings and Resources
You will need the following readings and resources for the course: The Bible (NASB, ESV, NRSV, NIV, or NLT) J. D. Harvey, *A Commentary on Romans* [ISBN: 9780825442100]

The ninth and final step in defining a course is to *allocate workload and grade weighting*. The US Department of Education provides the following guidance regarding the definition of a credit hour: "One hour of classroom or direct faculty instruction and a minimum of two hours of out-of-class student work each week for approximately fifteen weeks for one semester or trimester hour of credit, or ten to twelve weeks for one quarter hour of credit, or the equivalent amount of work over a different amount of time."[15] A simple way of stating workload for courses that meet during a semester is that students engage in forty-five hours of study per credit hour (three hours of study per week over fifteen weeks).

That parameter carries across all levels of instruction—undergraduate, graduate, and advanced. It is important to note that the workload hours include both in-class and out-of-class work. So, a fifteen-week three-credit course will involve approximately 45 hours in class and 90 hours outside of class for a total of 135 hours of student workload. It is also worth keeping in mind that, although an educational "hour" consists of fifty minutes, it is most effective simply to calculate total workload as 135 hours rather than 6,750 minutes (i.e., 135 x 50). Of course, some residential courses might meet in class for more than three hours during the week, and most likely online courses will have minimal "class time." Regardless of modality, though, the total hours of student workload for a three-credit course remains at 135.

For the sake of class members, it is important to calculate their workload realistically. Appendix B provides one set of workload parameters that should prove to be helpful in that regard. Since it is better to overestimate the time required for an assignment than to underestimate it, the table is on the conservative side. A number of universities provide online course workload estimators, including Rice University and Wake Forest University. The following table allocates workload for each assignment (or set of similar assignments) and correlates the time involved with the grade weighting for the Romans course that serves as the example in this chapter:

Assignments, Workload, and Grade Weighting		
Reading (380 pages)	35 hours	23%
Learning Tasks (35 class sessions)	35 hours	23%
Exegetical Practices (4)	40 hours	24%
Synthetic Study	10 hours	10%
Practical Project	10 hours	10%
Preparation and Oral Final Exam	5 hours	10%
Total	135 hours	100%

---

15. Code of Federal Regulations, 34 CFR § 600.2 Definitions.

Conclusion

A learning-centered approach to course design moves from goals to instruction, gives priority to learning, and focuses on assessing the degree to which learners achieve goals related to the topic they are studying. The key to designing a course is defining it. The process of defining a course, therefore, begins by describing typical learners and drafting a course description. After identifying the goals that class members should achieve by the end of the course, assign those goals to units within the course. Then, determine the assignments that will measure learning, and align those assignments with unit goals. Finally, select readings and resources and allocate workload and grade weighting across the assignments. The following pages set out an example of a completed course definition template. The course definition becomes the basis for designing the course syllabus.

Food for Thought
Can you think of a learning-centered course that you have experienced? What was your impression of the course?
To what extent do your current courses focus more on learning than on content coverage?
What is one course you teach that might adapt well to a learning-centered approach?
When might you set aside time to redefine that course using the model set out in this chapter?

Definition for a Biblical Studies Course on Paul's Letter to the Romans

Typical Learners
Typical learners will be at least twenty-five years old. Two-thirds are married, working full time, and studying part time. They have completed a previous baccalaureate degree, but only one in three has completed a previous degree in biblical-theological studies. Their level of biblical-theological knowledge varies widely as does the anticipated next step in their professional lives. All have some work and/or ministry experience. As members of Generation Z, they tend to prefer learning-centered strategies, such as case studies, gamification, or other experiential activities over passive activities such as lectures.

Course Description
In this course, you will focus on the New Testament's most organized, thorough exposition of Christian faith and its implications for Christian living. You will give special attention to the personal application of the message and will apply principles of biblical interpretation to the study of this letter.

Course Goals		
By the end of this course, you will have	Domain	Level
1. Assessed evidence related to the Introductory Questions for Romans.	Content	2
2. Created a graphic overview of the content, argument, and themes of Romans.	Competence	3
3. Interpreted selected passages in Romans using sound hermeneutical principles.	Competence	3
4. Discussed how biblical teachings from Romans apply to your own life.	Character	2
5. Outlined in detail the argument of Romans.	Content	1
6. Developed a plan for leading others through a study of Romans.	Competence	3

Unit #1—Grasping the Big Picture of Romans	
Goals: By the end of this unit, you will have	Assignments
1a Assessed evidence related to the Introductory Questions for Romans.	Learning task on Romans 1:1–17 and 15:14—16:27
1b Created a graphic overview of the content, argument, and themes of Romans.	Synthetic study

Unit #2—Interpreting and Applying Romans 1–4 The Revelation of God's Righteousness	
Goals: By the end of this unit, you will have	Assignments
2a Discussed how biblical teachings from Romans apply to your life.	Learning tasks on Romans 1:1—4:25

2b Interpreted selected passages in Romans using sound hermeneutical principles.	Exegetical practice on Romans 3:21–26

Unit #3—Interpreting and Applying Romans 5–8
The Demonstration of God's Power

Goals: By the end of this unit, you will have	Assignments
3a Discussed how biblical teachings from Romans apply to your life.	Learning tasks on Romans 5:1—8:39
3b Interpreted selected passages in Romans using sound hermeneutical principles.	Exegetical practice on Romans 8:12–17

Unit #4—Interpreting and Applying Romans 9–11
The Fulfillment of God's Plan

Goals: By the end of this unit, you will have	Assignments
4a Discussed how biblical teachings from Romans apply to your life.	Learning tasks on Romans 9:1—11:36
4b Interpreted selected passages in Romans using sound hermeneutical principles.	Exegetical practice on Romans 10:14–21

Unit #5—Interpreting and Applying Romans 12–16
The Transformation of God's People

Goals: By the end of this unit, you will have	Assignments
5a Discussed how biblical teachings from Romans apply to your life.	Learning tasks on Romans 12:1—16:27
5b Interpreted selected passages in Romans using sound hermeneutical principles.	Exegetical practice on Romans 15:14–21

Unit #6—Capturing and Communicating the Message of Romans

Goals: By the end of this unit, you will have	Assignments
6a Developed a plan for leading others through a study of Romans.	Practical project
6b Outlined in detail the argument of Romans.	Final exam

Readings and Resources
You will need the following readings and resources for the course: The Bible (NASB, ESV, NRSV, NIV, or NLT) J. D. Harvey, *A Commentary on Romans* [ISBN: 9780825442100]

Assignments, Workload, and Grade Weighting		
Reading (380 pages)	35 hours	23%
Learning Tasks (35 class sessions)	35 hours	23%
Exegetical Practices (4)	40 hours	24%
Synthetic Study	10 hours	10%
Practical Project	10 hours	10%
Preparation and Oral Final Exam	5 hours	10%
Total	135 hours	100%

4

Guiding the Learning: The Value of an Engaging Syllabus

Chapter Preview

A learning-centered approach to syllabus design provides a clear and organized framework for learning. The syllabus becomes a tool for the educator to foster engagement and enhance learning.

This approach ensures that the syllabus is more than a document of policies—it becomes a tool that aligns course goals, expectations, and resources to promote learner success.

Key elements of a learning-centered syllabus include: (1) welcoming the learner to the course, (2) introducing the course and educator in a way that fosters engagement and understanding, (3) providing a plan for learning through the course structure and schedule, (4) outlining course assignments, and (5) detailing expectations and policies for learners in a way that fosters engagement.

THE GOAL IS LEARNING, and an engaging syllabus is a valuable component of facilitating meaningful learning. Designing a course syllabus, however, presents a special challenge. Often, the educator inherits an established syllabus from, sometimes, generations of previous instructors. Other times, the educator encounters the daunting task of creating a syllabus from scratch that must comply with the institution's standards and expectations while clearly and coherently outlining course requirements. In either instance, learners can become lost in the process.

A syllabus serves a number of functions; in a learning-centered approach, the educator focuses on keeping learning as the ultimate goal of a well-designed syllabus. A syllabus can reinforce learning goals and build rapport and connection with learners. Traditionally, educators have viewed the syllabus from several perspectives.

Syllabus as Administrative Tool

Developing a syllabus requires attention to several constituents and stakeholders. These stakeholders often view the syllabus as primarily serving an administrative function for the college or university.[1] Externally, accreditors look to the syllabus to verify educational consistency and quality, while other institutions use the syllabus to confirm transfer equivalencies. Internally, deans or program directors review course syllabi as an accountability measure of their faculty members. Often, this administrative oversight leaves faculty members writing the syllabus to satisfy these concerns.

The syllabus also includes essential policies that ultimately come into question when justifying a learner's final grade in a course. Educators can easily form syllabi to defend against student grievances or grade appeals. In a study of faculty perspectives on the course syllabus, faculty members reported that administrative function or procedural matters are the primary role of the syllabus.[2] Although all of these functions are valid and appropriate syllabus uses, a learning-centered approach aims to go beyond the syllabus as an administrative tool.

Syllabus as Contract

A popular approach to the syllabus is to consider it a contract between instructor and student. In McKeachie's influential work, he adopts this approach as his primary model to describe the role of a syllabus.[3] Although a syllabus can serve as a means to communicate expectations and even imply a level of agreement from the student, the syllabus is not an enforceable contract. Furthermore, an educator who views the syllabus as a contract might create a business or transactional dynamic in the relationship with learners,

---

1. Eberly et al., "Syllabus as a Tool," 57.
2. Marcis et al., "Faculty Views," 189.
3. McKeachie and Svinicki, *Teaching Tips*, 21.

ultimately impeding learning.⁴ Wasley argues, "A syllabus bloated with legalese and a laundry list of dos and don'ts has turned the teacher-student relationship into an adversarial one."⁵ Although understanding the syllabus as a type of contract has value because it emphasizes the document's significance and the mutual understanding, respect, and agreement necessary in a productive learning environment, the contract model is insufficient in capturing the full potential of a motivational syllabus.

Syllabus as Road Map

The model for a syllabus most closely aligned with a learning-centered approach is the syllabus as a road map. In this model, the educator focuses on the learning goals and guides learners through the requirements to reach the desired learning goals. Often, this approach focuses on course design as the essential and primary emphasis of the syllabus. Focusing on learning goals raises the faculty member's "awareness regarding the impact of student engagement and student agency."⁶ This model for developing course syllabi provides a helpful framework for both the educator and the learner.

Syllabus as a Multifunctional Tool

All of these approaches to the syllabus contain helpful elements, but no single approach sufficiently captures the essential elements of a well-designed syllabus. Harrington and Thomas offer a threefold construct for a syllabus.⁷ They indicate three primary functions of the syllabus:

Communication Tool	Planning Tool	Motivational and Supportive Tool
A means to communicate the educator's expectations and philosophy.	A means to outline the goals of the course and the assignments and tasks that accomplish those goals.	A means to provide support and motivation, through resources outlined and purposes given.

---

4. Harrington and Thomas, *Motivational Syllabus*, 6.
5. Wasley, "Syllabus Becomes a Repository," para. 10.
6. Katsampoxaki-Hodgetts, "'Naked' Syllabus," 460.
7. Harrington and Thomas, *Motivational Syllabus*, 8.

By approaching the syllabus as a multifunctional tool to support learning, the educator includes all essential elements and meets stakeholder expectations, but ultimately, learning remains the primary driver.

Syllabus as a Communication Tool

As the different syllabus models above acknowledge, the syllabus provides a valuable opportunity for the educator to communicate with class members. Stepping back and considering how the learner will receive and understand a syllabus helps the educator consider how the learner will understand and digest the content. Three factors are important in viewing a syllabus as a communication tool.

Setting clear expectations is important. A syllabus is often the learner's earliest introduction both to the course content and to the educator. The syllabus should be available for college and university students before the first class session. At the very least, it is customary for the educator to begin the first class by introducing the syllabus. The syllabus then serves a critical role in defining expectations for how the learner and educator will relate during the course.

The syllabus is the official means by which the university communicates critical policies—for grading, attendance, and participation. The educator also outlines the schedule of assignments and deadlines. Communicating these policies clearly and concisely can make a difference in how learners understand their role in the course.

Whether the educator communicates these policies and expectations in a supportive and positive way influences the learning environment they establish. For example, many educators will have a policy on technology use in the classroom. The difference between begrudging compliance and willing participation is how the syllabus communicates expectations. See the examples of cell phone use policies below:

Two Cell Phone Policies
Use of Cell Phones
Cell phones are strictly prohibited in the classroom. Unauthorized cell phone use will result in immediate expulsion from the class session (absence will be recorded). Unauthorized use includes texting, web searches, or making calls. Repeated offenses might result in further disciplinary action. The use of cell phones disrupts the instructor and the classroom as a whole. I expect class members to keep their phones off or on silent and out of sight during class. I will only consider exceptions for documented emergencies or approved accommodations.

> **Use of Cell Phones**
>
> Please help support an engaging learning environment in our classroom by silencing or turning off your cell phone when you are in class. A cell phone-free space allows everyone to be fully present, engaged with the material, and respect the shared learning experience.
>
> If you anticipate an exceptional circumstance (e.g., family emergencies or work responsibilities that require accessibility), please communicate them to me before class. I am happy to work with you to find a way both to support our classroom environment and to meet your needs.
>
> Sometimes, we use cell phones for activities such as accessing online resources or participating in interactive polls. Otherwise, I encourage you to view our class time as an opportunity to disconnect and focus on meaningful engagement.

These two examples establish the roles and dynamics the learner can expect. Both policies communicate expectations. Both policies also communicate an environment and class culture. The second policy approaches communicating expectations as an opportunity to communicate values and establish a supportive, learning-focused relationship.

Maintaining a student-centered focus is also important. When preparing a syllabus, educators often focus on their own priorities and needs. An effective syllabus also considers the learner's perspective, always asking, "How will this approach promote learning?" Asking at every opportunity, "How will class members understand or receive the material?"

A learning-centered focus will consider the specific learners in the course. Knowing the audience means considering the learner's level (undergraduate? Or graduate? Or advanced?), assumptions about familiarity with the subject matter, and educational background. For example, a classroom (whether physical or virtual) full of doctoral students will mean a high level of academic experience. These experienced learners will come with their own assumptions about the role of the instructor and appropriate classroom etiquette. No matter who the learners are, it is the educator's responsibility to seek to understand how they will receive and understand the content. Also, will the way in which the instructor presents the content motivate the learners?

Using visuals is also important. Although the strategies to create a student-centered syllabus are as varied as the learners themselves, an effective approach is to move beyond a text-based syllabus and consider how to illustrate content. Nilson argues that a syllabus that communicates must move beyond text alone.[8] She provides a guide for a graphic syllabus and mapping outcomes as an alternative to the text-based syllabus. She argues that visuals grab learners' attention more effectively than dense paragraphs of text,

---

8. Nilson. *Graphic Syllabus*, 8.

allowing the educator to illustrate connections and logic that strengthen and clarify the content and assessments. Consider the following examples. The first is a text-based version of the assessment for an Action Research course:

Assessment

1. Participation (10%)
2. Literature Review (15%)
3. Action Research Proposal (20%)
4. Data Collection Report (20%)
5. Final Project and Presentation (30%)
6. Reflection Journal (5%)

The second is a graphic version for the same course.

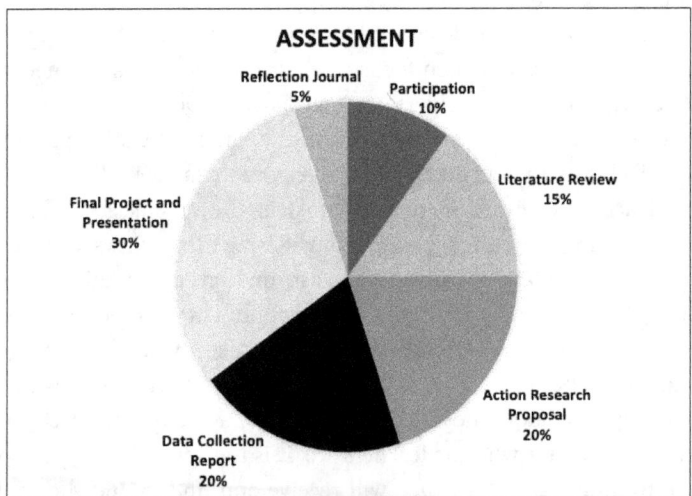

This graphic version draws the learners' attention to the same content. Not only are class members more likely to stop and focus on the graphic representation of the information, but the graphic also underscores the significance and weight of each assignment. Highlighting important elements within the syllabus by using creative graphics and formatting emphasizes both the importance of the content and the value of learner comprehension. Including content in a table rather than in a paragraph is another simple way to clarify and emphasize specific content. Here is an example that combines workload with assessment:

Assignment	Workload	Evaluation
Reading	25 hours	—
Participation: Engaged dialogue and discussions	10 hours	10%
Literature Review: Depth of research and synthesis	20 hours	15%
Action Research Proposal: Clarity and feasibility	20 hours	20%
Data Collection Report: Quality of analysis	20 hours	20%
Final Project and Presentation: Application of research	30 hours	30%
Reflection Journal: Critical insights	10 hours	5%
Total	135 hours	100%

Since learners increasingly access syllabi digitally rather than by a printed copy, using color and images offers new possibilities to amplify and capture their interest. Using visuals also provides an opportunity to consider the type of course the educator is teaching. A course in digital media, for instance, might include more creative elements than other subject matters. The ability to connect subject matter creatively to the syllabus presentation demonstrates the educator's passion for the subject matter.

Including visuals and graphics in a syllabus might seem overwhelming for many educators. The key is to look for opportunities to communicate more effectively with the learner. A graphic could just as easily be a distraction for the learner. As with any teaching method, constantly considering the learner, seeking feedback, and continuously improving methods are critical. The syllabus is another tool for teaching and deserves the same attention as other teaching methods.

Syllabus as a Planning Tool

The syllabus also serves as an essential planning tool, both for the educator and the learner. The syllabus structures the learning so that learners can see the full scope of the course while outlining the individual components in digestible, intuitive stages.

Earlier chapters provide specifics for structuring the course and developing a course definition. The educator builds the framework of the course into the course definition, and the syllabus guides the learner through that structure, providing flow and context to each element.

One of the key elements in both a course definition and a course syllabus is the articulation of course goals. Course goals relate directly to the content of the course, but they also serve as guideposts for learning. Writing goals in straightforward, clear, learner-friendly language ensures that they are meaningful for both the educator and the learner.

Creating a motivational, learning-centered syllabus also means developing course goals that address cognitive, affective, and behavioral domains. By varying the focus of the goal to different learning domains, the educator acknowledges the learner as a whole person and avoids treating teaching and learning only as transactional. The following table illustrates clear, understandable learning goals as well as the domains of learning reflected in the goals of a syllabus in Action Research:

	Student Learning Goal	Domains of Learning	Verifying Learning
Goal 1	Develop research questions to address a meaningful problem in education.	Cognitive: Application and analysis of real-world challenges.	Research problem statement.
Goal 2	Design a study using action research methods.	Cognitive: Synthesis and planning. Behavioral: Creating research designs.	Literature review and in-class research design tasks.
Goal 3	Collect and interpret quantitative and qualitative data.	Cognitive: Analysis of data. Behavioral: Using research tools.	Data analysis assignment.
Goal 4	Create an action plan based on research findings.	Cognitive: Evaluation and problem-solving. Affective: Commitment to improving practice.	Action plan assignments and classroom discussions.
Goal 5	Communicate research findings effectively.	Cognitive: Communication. Affective: Appreciating audience response.	Workshop tasks and report submissions.
Goal 6	Reflect on the action research process.	Cognitive: Critical thinking/evaluation. Affective: Valuing self-assessment and continuous improvement.	Final presentation and peer feedback.

Learners of all ages and levels ask, "So what?" The syllabus allows the educator to anticipate and answer that question. Learners are most likely motivated not just by the joy of learning (as teachers often hope and dream) but also by the future outcome of that learning in completing their degree and all that comes with that achievement. So, course goals take on greater meaning when the educator connects learning to program outcomes and career outcomes. The following table is an expanded version of learning goals connecting each course goal to broader program goals needed for a career in education:

	Student Learning Goal	**How does this outcome help me become a better educator and leader?**
Goal 1	Develop research questions to address a meaningful problem in education.	Defining problems clearly and asking good questions leads to more effective solutions. These skills are critical for curriculum design, policy development, and instructional leadership.
Goal 2	Design a study using action research methods.	Designing a solid research plan prepares you for data-driven decision-making and strategic planning. These are key components of school leadership and professional development roles.
Goal 3	Collect and interpret quantitative and qualitative data.	Effectively collecting data and interpreting this data will be an ongoing need in any role in educational leadership.
Goal 4	Create an action plan based on research findings.	Implementing a plan from research results is what makes the educational leader a change agent in his or her context.
Goal 5	Communicate research findings effectively.	Explaining research is crucial for sharing insights with teachers, administrators, parents, and policymakers. The best research can be ignored or misunderstood without this skill to communicate findings effectively.
Goal 6	Reflect on the action research process.	Thinking critically about your research experience makes you a more empathetic and caring leader.

By making these connections explicit, learners can see how the knowledge and skills that they gain in this course translate directly to their professional growth and future impact.

Syllabus as an Organizational Tool

The syllabus should bring clarity to both the course details and to the bigger picture of the course. A well-designed syllabus reinforces the flow and rhythms of the course, making the learning intuitive and logical. Learners often look to the course schedule and the course requirements/assessments as the essential aspects of the syllabus. So, the educator might choose to incorporate elements to reinforce course goals.

Unit	Week	Topic/Learning Tasks	Assignments Submit by: Friday 11:59 p.m.
Unit 1: Foundations of Action Research	1	Ethical considerations	
	2	Brainstorming research topics	
	3	Peer review of problem statements	**Problem Statement**
Unit 2: Designing the Research Study	4	Quantitative research methods Activity: Develop research questions	
	5	Quantitative research methods Activity: Analyze literature reviews	
	6	Discussion: Ethical considerations in data collection	**Literature Review**
Unit 3: Collecting and Analyzing Data	7	Workshop: Design surveys and interview questions	
	8	Case Study Analysis: Sample data sets	
	9	Workshop: Code qualitative data	**Data Collection Analysis Plan**
Unit 4: Action Plan and Communication	10	Group Discussion: Action plan strategies	
	11	Writing Workshop: Structure a research report	
	12	Activity: Mock presentations and feedback	
	13	Workshop: Refine research projects	**Action Plan**

	14	Class Presentations	
Unit 5: Implementation and Reflection	15	Class Presentations	
	16	Peer Review: Feedback on projects	**Final Project**

Graphics offer an engaging alternative to an entirely text-based syllabus. Often, course goals and structure are the educator's primary focus, but learners miss them entirely. Creating a diagram to illustrate the structure and goals of the course can serve as a valuable discipline for educators. They can address the challenge of logical gaps or extraneous information by converting the content into a chart or visual that depicts the logic and organization of the content.[9] For the learner, a visual aid can clarify and simplify what can be dense and difficult to comprehend.

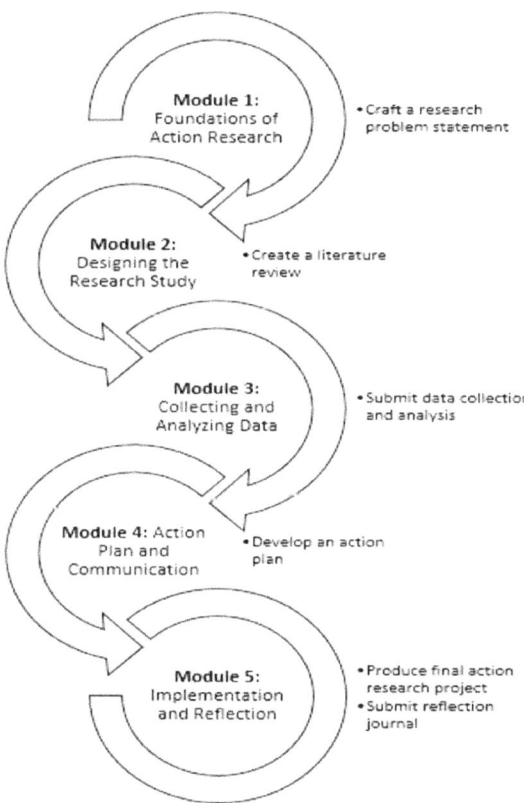

9. Nilson. *Graphic Syllabus*, 88.

Syllabus as a Motivational and Supportive Tool

Traditional textbooks are often an early consideration when choosing required learning materials for a course. The materials required for a course are a starting point and will serve as the learner's primary resource for learning. As subject-matter experts, educators might choose texts that were most meaningful in their own educational background. Again, the learning-centered syllabus takes a different approach. The educator faces the challenge of thinking about which texts, readings, or even multimedia will lead most effectively to learning. A traditional textbook still might be the best choice for a course, but the learning-focused educator looks beyond only a required text and considers other resources that will enhance learning. Including additional resources in the syllabus provides the learner with recommendations for further exploration and research. Emphasizing accessibility and inclusivity in resource selection underpins the classroom culture.

The syllabus is also meaningful for highlighting *support services* such as tutoring, writing centers, and mental health resources. Administrative areas at most universities and colleges have outreach plans to encourage using their services; the educator is an additional voice to encourage using these resources. The syllabus is another opportunity to reduce apprehension about using these services by highlighting potential support services. Learners are often aware of services, but the syllabus can provide additional motivation to utilize these supports.

The educator might incorporate *tips and ideas for success* in the course that go beyond university resources such as tutoring. By including tips for success, the educator communicates empathy and interest in the unique challenges the learners will face. A freshman undergraduate course might include tips about note-taking in class or healthy sleep patterns. A graduate or doctoral class might benefit from tips for balancing work, family, or ministry responsibilities with the course workload. Often, the specific tips are less important than the fact that the educator seeks to connect with learners in supportive and meaningful ways.

The educator can also frame all the necessary syllabus elements with an eye to *tone and transparency*. A pitfall is to focus on the necessary elements of a syllabus and present policies and required elements in a contractual, transactional tone. The educator can gain valuable insights by inviting a learner to read and provide feedback on the overall flow and tone of the syllabus. Tone can make all the difference in inspiring curiosity and a sense of purpose. By using an inviting and supportive tone and language, the educator builds rapport and establishes a welcoming culture that extends into the virtual or physical classroom.

Syllabus Outline and Checklist

The flow of the syllabus follows the needs of the learner. In the broadest terms, the following list provides a helpful *syllabus outline*:

Syllabus Outline

1. Welcome the Student
2. Overview of the Course
3. Introduce the Instructor
4. Explain Course Structure and Schedule
5. Clarify Assignment Details
6. Establish Policies and Expectations

Using this outline as a starting point, the educator then incorporates each of the elements listed in the checklist below. This checklist serves as a helpful tool for all required elements and guiding questions to consider when formulating the tone and focus for each element:

Guiding Questions	Checklist	
Communication		
Setting Clear Expectations • What policies are essential to a productive learning environment? • What policies are essential to student learning? • What policies are required by the college/university?	*Attendance* *Use of technology* *Plagiarism/academic integrity* *Artificial intelligence* *Late work*	☐ ☐ ☐ ☐ ☐
Focusing on Learning • How will this approach promote learning? • How will students understand or receive the material? • Can I add a visual (graphic, table, etc.) to communicate more effectively?	*Instructor contact information* *Course description* *Form and style guidelines* *Course workload* *Course evaluation* *Grading scale*	☐ ☐ ☐ ☐ ☐ ☐

Planning		
Connecting Objectives • Are the course objectives diversified in learning domains and levels? • How are the course objectives connected to program and career outcomes?	*Course objectives* *Course requirements*	☐ ☐
Structuring the Course • Does the course have a predictable rhythm? • Is workload distributed in the course?	*Course schedule* *Course workload*	☐ ☐
Motivation and Support		
Providing Resources • Are required course materials identified? • Are support services such as tutoring, writing centers, and mental health resources listed? • Are other readings and resources listed?	*Required course materials* *Resources* *Bibliography* *Office hours/contact information*	☐ ☐ ☐ ☐
Establishing Tone and Transparency • Have I considered how to inspire curiosity and a sense of purpose? • Are my tone and language inviting and supportive?	*Instructor welcome* *Personal introduction*	☐ ☐

The checklist serves as a tool not only for creating a syllabus but also for revising a syllabus. With each offering of a course, the educator has the opportunity to *assess and revise the syllabus*. In adapting the syllabus with each use, educators should also consider the overall length of the syllabus. They should aim to communicate concisely and clearly, allowing the necessary syllabus elements to determine the ideal length for a syllabus. The temptation might be to continue to add content to the syllabus. When the educator aims to engage the learner with the syllabus, however, a bloated, lengthy syllabus is not an option. With each iteration of the syllabus, astute educators will identify unique needs and adapt the syllabus for those specific learners. They will also seek to streamline and simplify whenever possible to increase readability.

Tips for Engaging Students with the Syllabus

A well-crafted syllabus is only effective if learners use it. An educator inadvertently diminishes the significance of the syllabus by posting the syllabus on the course site in the learning management system (LMS) and continuing with the course. Educators end up constantly referring to the syllabus as learners pepper them with questions that a quick check of the syllabus could easily resolve. The educator reduces questions and confusion throughout the course by utilizing creative approaches to introducing the syllabus.

Faculty members resist investing energy and time in developing the syllabus when learners ignore it. Although some learners might be sufficiently motivated, typical learners (usually at the undergraduate level) are unlikely to initiate a deep dive into the syllabus without some extrinsic motivation. Some strategies to encourage engagement with the syllabus include a syllabus scavenger hunt, a syllabus quiz, and syllabus reflection.

A *syllabus scavenger hunt* can help engage class members by challenging them to find important policies and elements. Here is an example of a syllabus scavenger hunt:

Syllabus Scavenger Hunt
Due Dates and Schedule
• When is the first assignment date?
• What are the latest day and time to submit an assignment?
Grading and Assessment
• What assignments are worth 20 percent of your grade?
• What is your grade if your final average is 94.1?
Policies and Expectations
• What is the policy regarding late work?
• What is the policy regarding artificial intelligence?
Resources and Materials
• What is the required textbook for the course?
• What supplementary materials does the syllabus mention?
Contact Information
• What is the most reliable way to reach me?
• How can you make an appointment with me?

Break the learners into pairs and offer an incentive for the group that finishes first and has the correct answers. This approach would reinforce not only the information found in the syllabus but also the importance and priority of the syllabus itself.

Giving learners a *syllabus quiz* is another helpful strategy for reinforcing the significance of the syllabus. Similar to the scavenger hunt, a quiz on the syllabus's content during the course's introduction emphasizes both the information and the value of the syllabus. The educator might deliver the quiz live in class using a tool like Kahoot! or through the LMS. A syllabus quiz delivered as an in-class activity can create interest and positive energy within the class, thus serving the additional use of building a positive classroom culture.

An in-class learning task that asks learners to engage in *syllabus reflection* can prompt them to read the syllabus and reflect on their own goals, questions, or concerns for the course. They can share their reflections with classmates within the class or simply submit them for the educator to review. A syllabus reflection activity not only emphasizes the importance of the syllabus by designating instructional time toward its review, but the educator can gain valuable insights into both the learners and the effectiveness of the syllabus.

Although these examples showcase creative ways to help learners engage the syllabus, many intentional strategies can be effective. The key is that if the syllabus is important to the educator, then the educator will ensure that the syllabus is important to the learner.

Conclusion

Even after decades of evolving practices in education, the syllabus remains an essential tool for the educator and the learner. The educator must approach the syllabus with the same intentionality as any other educational practice. At every opportunity, the educator must return to the syllabus as a living document that evolves with the needs of the learners. This chapter surveys best practices in developing a syllabus, but no syllabus is ever complete. Every year, the needs of learners change, and educators learn how to communicate more effectively through the syllabus. By encouraging feedback from learners and colleagues, the educator can embrace continually improving the syllabus for greater impact and effectiveness.

Food for Thought
How did you approach the syllabus before reading this chapter? Administrative tool? Contract? Road map?
Evaluate a course syllabus from a course you either have taken or have taught. How have these principles been incorporated?
What is one principle from this chapter that you can apply to a syllabus for a course that you teach?
When is your next opportunity to use the syllabus checklist to revise a syllabus for a course that you teach?

Sample Syllabus

COLLEGE
LOGO

EDU 501
Action Research for Educators
Fall Semester Course (16 weeks)
Classroom Building | Tuesday/Thursday
10:00 a.m.–11:15 a.m.

WELCOME

Instructor Headshot

Welcome to Action Research for Educators! Action research is a practical tool for educators, helping you identify challenges, analyze data, and implement meaningful change in classrooms and schools. This course will equip you with practical skills to explore real-world issues and develop actionable solutions.

COURSE DESCRIPTION

You will learn practical research skills to improve teaching and learning. You will identify problems, collect and analyze data, and develop research-based solutions for real-world educational settings. Emphasis is placed on critical reflection, collaborative inquiry, and effective communication to drive meaningful change in schools and classrooms.

RELATION TO THE ACADEMIC PROGRAM

This course supports the MEd program by equipping educators with research, problem-solving, and data-informed decision-making skills. This course reinforces educational leadership, reflective practice, and continuous improvement, empowering students to analyze challenges, implement solutions, and drive meaningful change in their classrooms, schools, and educational organizations.

COURSE INSTRUCTOR

My twenty years of experience as a teacher and administrator have shaped my commitment to data-informed decision-making, reflective practice, and continual improvement (all essential elements of action research!). I know the challenges that teachers and administrators faced, I also know how helpless you can feel to face those challenges. Action research gives you the tools to face those problems systematically and strategically and to bring about real change in a classroom or institution.

CONTACT INFORMATION

Please contact me throughout the course, particularly as questions arise. It is better to ask about something you do not understand than to wander about in uncertainty. I am available during regular university hours in my office located in the Faculty Building. The most reliable way to reach me is by email. I will do my best to respond within twenty-four hours. If a conversation would be helpful, please use my calendar link to find a time: https://calendar/instructorname.

    Email: instructorname@college.edu
    Office Phone: (xxx) xxx-xxxx

COURSE OUTCOMES

We will walk through every action research component, developing your confidence and effectiveness in utilizing research to make meaningful changes in education practices. By the end of our course together, you will have done the following:

- Developed research questions to address a meaningful problem in education.
- Designed a study using action research methods.
- Collected and interpreted quantitative and qualitative data.
- Created an action plan based on research findings.
- Communicated research findings effectively.
- Reflected on the action research process.

COURSE TEXTBOOK

Mills, G. E., and L. R. Gay. *Educational Research: Competencies for Analysis and Applications*. 12th ed. Pearson, 2019.

COURSE WORKLOAD AND EVALUATION

Assignment	Workload	Evaluation
Reading	25 hours	—
Participation: Engaged dialogue and discussions	10 hours	10%
Literature Review: Depth of research and synthesis	20 hours	15%
Action Research Proposal: Clarity and feasibility	20 hours	20%
Data Collection Report: Quality of analysis	20 hours	20%
Final Project and Presentation: Application of research	30 hours	30%
Reflection Journal: Critical insights	10 hours	5%
Total	135 hours	100%

COURSE ASSIGNMENT DETAILS

Participation: Actively contribute to in-class discussions, demonstrate critical thinking, and engage with peers in meaningful conversations about action research concepts. (Ongoing; assessed based on the quality of contributions, preparedness, and engagement in weekly discussions.)

Literature Review: Research and synthesize relevant literature to provide a foundation for your action research project, demonstrating a clear understanding of existing studies and best practices. (2,000–2,500 words; minimum eight to ten scholarly sources in Turabian format.)

Action Research Proposal: Develop a well-structured proposal outlining your research problem, methodology, and intended outcomes, ensuring feasibility and alignment with action research principles. (1,500–2,000 words; includes problem statement, research questions, methodology, and expected impact.)

Data Collection Report: Collect, organize, and analyze qualitative and/or quantitative data, interpreting findings to assess their relevance to your research question. (1,500–2,000 words; includes data sources, analysis methods, and preliminary findings.)

Final Project and Presentation: Compile your research findings into a comprehensive report and deliver a presentation demonstrating how your study contributes to educational improvement. (Final paper: 3,500–4,000 words; Presentation: ten-to-fifteen minutes with visual aids.)

Reflection Journal: Regularly reflect on your research journey, documenting key insights, challenges, and personal growth. (Five journal entries; 300–500 words each.)

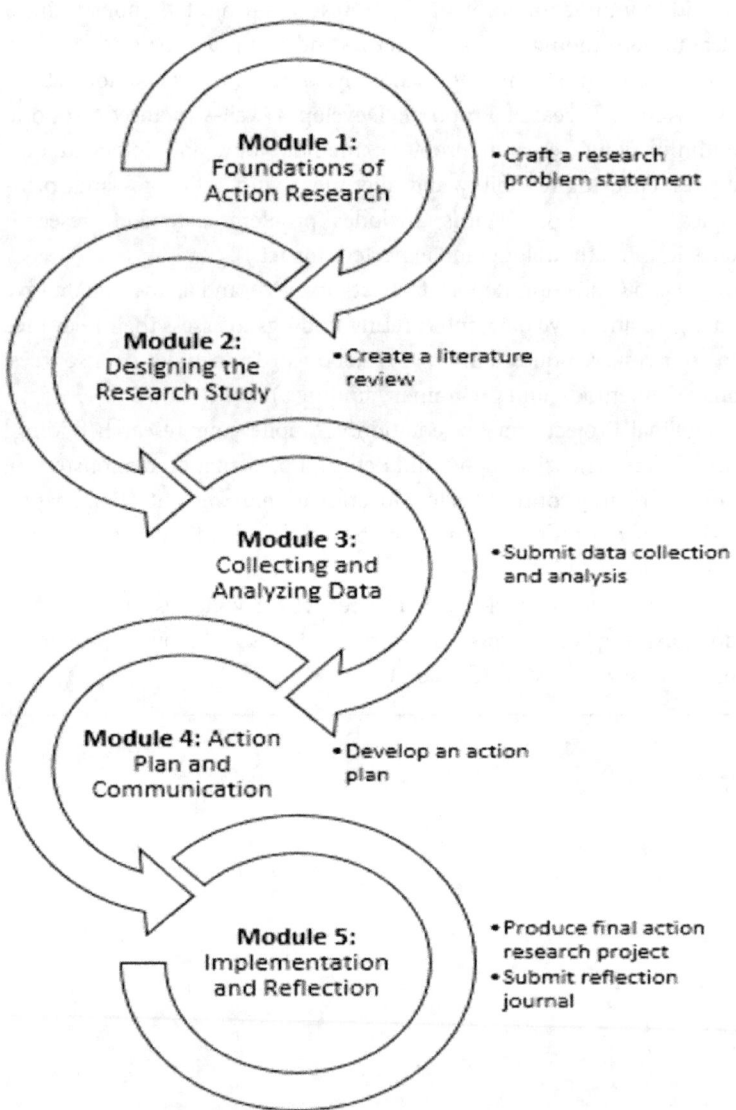

Course Schedule

		Topic/Learning Tasks	Assignments (Last day to submit: Friday 11:59 p.m.)
Module 1: Foundations of Action Research	Week 1	Ethical considerations	
	Week 2	Brainstorming research topics	
	Week 3	Peer review of problem statements	**Submit problem statement**
Module 2: Designing the Research Study	Week 4	Quantitative research methods In-Class Exercise: Developing research questions	
	Week 5	Quantitative research methods Activity: Analyzing sample literature reviews	
	Week 6	Discussion: Ethical considerations in data collection	**Submit literature review**
Module 3: Collecting and Analyzing Data	Week 7	Workshop: Designing surveys and interview questions	
	Week 8	Case Study Analysis: Sample data sets	
	Week 9	Workshop: Coding qualitative data	**Submit data collection and analysis plan**
Module 4: Action Plan and Communication	Week 10	Group Discussion: Action plan strategies	
	Week 11	Writing Workshop: Structuring a research report	
	Week 12	Activity: Mock presentations and feedback	
	Week 13	Workshop: Refining research projects	**Submit action plan**
Module 5: Implementation and Reflection	Week 14	Class Presentations	**Submit final project**
	Week 15	Class Presentations	
	Week 16	Peer Review: Feedback on projects	**Submit reflection journal**

FORM AND STYLE

Since Turabian formatting is essential for research writing, practicing these guidelines now will prepare you for scholarly work in this course and beyond. For additional support, refer to the College Stylesheet, and do not hesitate to ask if you need guidance!

- Use 12-point Times New Roman font, single-spacing, and one-inch margins to maintain readability and a professional appearance.
- Include a cover page with your name, assignment title, and submission date.
- Use Turabian formatting for all citations.
- Submit each assignment as a single PDF file to ensure accessibility and consistency.

ATTENDANCE

Your presence in class is essential, not only for your own learning but also for the success of our discussions and collaborative work. I will take attendance at every class meeting, and to receive full credit for participation, I expect you to attend regularly, come prepared, and engage actively in discussions.

If you need to miss a class for a permissible reason (such as illness), please notify me in advance whenever possible. Although these absences are understandable, they still count toward your overall attendance requirement.

Because this course is highly interactive, excessive absences will impact your grade. Students who miss more than 25 percent of class meetings will not be able to pass the course. If you encounter challenges that affect your ability to attend, please reach out—I want to help you stay engaged and successful in this course.

LATE WORK

Since timeliness is an important skill in both academic and professional settings, you should complete and submit all assignments on time. If you anticipate difficulty meeting a deadline, please communicate with me as soon as possible.

Late assignments will result in a 10 percent deduction per day. If extenuating circumstances arise, I encourage you to reach out—I will evaluate situations on a case-by-case basis.

I will not accept assignments after the official end date of the course. Any work submitted after the final class day will receive a grade of 0 unless I have approved an Incomplete grade in advance. To request an Incomplete, you must apply during the final month of the semester and have completed at least 50 percent of the coursework.

I understand that unexpected challenges can arise. I encourage you to manage deadlines proactively. I am happy to discuss options and help you stay on track!

GRADING SCALE

Grade	Percentage	Quality Points per Credit Hour
A	95–100	4.0
A-	92–94	3.7
B+	89–91	3.3
B	86–88	3.0
B-	83–85	2.7
C+	80–82	2.3
C	77–79	2.0
C-	74–76	1.7
D+	71–73	1.3
D	68–70	1.0
D-	65–67	0.7
F	0–64	0.0

ACADEMIC SUCCESS CENTER (ASC)—TUTORING AND ACCOMMODATIONS

We are committed to supporting your academic success. If you need tutoring, study resources, or assistance with writing and research, the Academic Success Center offers various services to help you excel. Whether you are looking for one-on-one tutoring, study strategies, or help in refining your assignments, our team is here to assist you.

For students needing disability accommodations, the Academic Success Center provides reasonable accommodations to ensure equal access to learning. If you have a documented disability or believe you might need support, please reach out as early as possible to discuss available resources.

For more information or to schedule an appointment, contact the Academic Success Center at [insert contact information]. We are here to help you succeed!

ACADEMIC INTEGRITY AND PLAGIARISM

Honesty, integrity, and original work are essential to learning and developing as a professional. Plagiarism, whether intentional or unintentional, is a violation of academic integrity. Students are responsible for learning and applying proper citation practices, and faculty members provide guidance through syllabi, course materials, and institutional resources.

Resources on avoiding plagiarism and correctly citing sources are readily available to support you in maintaining integrity in your writing. If you have questions about proper citation or attribution, please reach out for guidance—we are here to help you succeed.

The unauthorized use of artificial intelligence tools (e.g., ChatGPT) without instructor permission and proper acknowledgment is prohibited. Always check with your professor if you are unsure about AI use in coursework.

We hold academic graduate and doctoral students to the highest standard. Egregious acts of academic dishonesty or cheating might result in immediate dismissal from the university. If you ever have concerns about citations or research ethics, I encourage you to ask—we want to help you build confidence in your academic work.

COLLEGE EMAIL

I will send all email correspondence for this course to your official college email address. Please make it a habit to check your college email regularly for course announcements, feedback, and other important information. When reaching out about this course, be sure to send messages from your @college.edu account so that your emails are received and responded to promptly.

5

Assessing the Learning: The Rationale for Well-Designed Rubrics

Chapter Preview
Rubrics enhance learning by bringing clarity to the assessment process, both for the educator and for the learner.
Educators will find that a well-designed rubric improves communication by reinforcing learning goals and increasing transparency in assessment.
Rubrics remove the guesswork from the assessment process so that the focus remains on the learning.
Simple steps make developing a rubric possible for every educator: (1) define the criteria, (2) describe performance levels, and (3) assign values.

THE GOAL IS LEARNING, and it is important to know the extent to which learning is actually taking place. The educator spends countless hours carefully designing a course, developing an engaging syllabus, and creating an interactive classroom experience. All of these elements are essential to cultivating learning, but how can the educator be certain that class members are learning?

The answer is assessment in its variety of forms. According to Marzano, Pickering, and McTighe, "What we now know about learning indicates that assessment and learning are closely and intimately tied."[1] Not all assessments, however, are equal in measuring learning. If assignments are unclear or disconnected from learning goals, assessments can frustrate the learning process. Rubrics are the learning-centered educators' best tool for bringing transparency to the assessment process.

Rubrics find their origins, according to Selke, in red ink or red chalk.[2] In her explanation of the origins of rubrics, she connects rubrics with medieval manuscripts where scribes would include notations in red coloring as a way to indicate emphasis or specific directions to the reader. Not until the 1970s did the language of rubrics appear in education literature. In these years, educators utilized the language of rubrics to describe the levels of development in kindergarten through twelfth-grade students.

Finally, in the twenty-first century, educators adopted rubrics for use in post-secondary education. In recent decades, college educators have utilized rubrics to assess academic and nonacademic competencies, to enhance learning and teaching processes, and to document mastery of specific knowledge and skills. Even with the relatively recent adoption of rubrics, college and university educators go so far as to claim that rubrics are "the most effective grading devices since the invention of red ink."[3]

Rubrics Bring Clarity to the Assessment Process

Imagine walking into an exam completely unprepared, unsure of the topic, the format, or even what constitutes a passing grade. Such a situation would be a nightmare! Assessment without a clear rubric creates a similar experience for learners. Without clear criteria, learners might feel lost and uncertain about how their instructor will evaluate their work or how they will meet expectations.

In a learning-centered approach, the educator seeks to reinforce learning while also reducing confusion, frustration, or intimidation for class members. Rubrics are an integral part of the learning process. With rubrics, the educator pulls back the curtain on the assessment process. The educator involves the learner in this process, disclosing the intent and outcome of any assessment.

---

1. Marzano et al., *Assessing Student Outcomes*, 11.
2. Selke, *Rubric Assessment Goes to College*, xiv.
3. Stevens and Levi, *Introduction to Rubrics*, 3.

Rubrics Increase Confidence

Rubrics involve learners in the assessment process and show them exactly how to measure their work. By involving them in assessment with rubrics, the educator not only removes the stress of an ambiguous assessment but also builds the learner's confidence. The learning process is innately a frustrating one. Class members must move from being uncertain and even confused to a deeper level of understanding and proficiency. The wise educator seeks to create an environment that alleviates distraction and discouragement from this learning process so that class members can remain focused on learning.

An educator is constantly assessing learning. This assessment can be formal or informal, structured or free-form. The formal assessment that ultimately results in a final grade is often a source of anxiety for the learner. So, any time that the educator can increase transparency and build trust with class members, he or she fosters learning.

Rubrics draw learners into the assessment process. The educator's proverbial cards are on the table. Class members know not only what the educator expects them to learn and how the educator will verify that learning, but they also know that the educator will be accountable to those measures. When they understand the rules that they must follow to succeed, their confidence in the process expands. When they know the rules that the educator will follow, their trust in him or her increases.

Practical Steps for Creating Rubrics

Rubrics can be simple or complex. They can assess a variety of assignments. They can use a variety of approaches. As the history of rubrics demonstrates, educators first adopted rubrics in elementary education. Although educators have subsequently embraced the use of rubrics for higher levels of learning, the principles for designing effective rubrics apply equally to a kindergarten classroom and to a doctoral course. Rubric design follows a simple process that can apply to any form of assessment. It involves three steps:

1. Define the criteria.
2. Establish performance levels.
3. Develop descriptors.

The assignment of making a peanut butter and jelly sandwich illustrates the simplicity of the process. Although the task is simple, it requires multiple steps, allows for some variation, and applies to learners of all levels. The educator can create a rubric using these steps.

First, *define the criteria* by asking "What will I assess?" List any possible criteria for the task. Then, narrow the list to those criteria that will best demonstrate successful completion of the task. For the task of making a peanut butter and jelly sandwich, goals might be neatness, preparation, orderliness, efficiency, carefulness, and creativity. The educator lists the possible criteria for the task. After listing all possible criteria, the educator then considers which are primary and fully cover the aspects of the task. Although there is no limit to the number of criteria to include, simplicity is often helpful for both the educator and the learner. In this example, the educator might simplify the list to three criteria:

> *Example Criteria: Peanut Butter and Jelly Sandwich Assignment*
> **Preparation:** Did they select the right ingredients? Did they gather the right tools?
> **Process:** Did they follow logical steps? Did they include all necessary steps?
> **Presentation:** Is the final result neat and appetizing?

The criteria compose what Stevens and Levi call the "dimensions" of the rubric.[4] List them down the left-hand column of the rubric:

Preparation				
Process				
Presentation.				

Second, *establish performance levels* by asking "What are the different levels of performance?" The educator might simply want class members to accomplish the task without detailing levels of performance. In that case, the performance levels might simply be Complete or Incomplete. Often, however, the educator will want to provide more nuance to the possible performance levels and might choose levels such as Excellent, Good, Developing, and Needs Improvement. For the peanut butter and jelly example, the educator might choose to create labels for the performance levels that both communicate the level, but also reflect the nature of the assignment: Master Chef, Confident Cook, Learning to Cook, and Sticky Situation. Even without description, these levels provide clarity on the expectations for each level of performance. The performance levels compose what Stevens and

---

4. Stevens and Levi, *Introduction to Rubrics*, 10.

Levi call the "scale levels" of the rubric.[5] List them across the top row of the rubric:

	Master Chef	Confident Cook	Learning to Cook	Sticky Situation
Preparation				
Process				
Presentation				

Third, *develop descriptors* by asking "How do I define the different levels of performance?" In this step, the educator defines each of the performance levels for each of the criteria. Descriptors tell learners the particulars of what makes up the levels of performance. Class members can then use the descriptors to self-assess before they submit their assignment. The descriptors fill in the remaining cells of the rubric. Here is an example of a completed rubric for the peanut butter and jelly assignment:

Assignment: Making a Peanut Butter and Jelly Sandwich
Description: Prepare, produce, and present a PB&J sandwich that is complete, neat, and fun to eat.
Purpose: To gain experience in the art of sandwich making.

	Master Chef	Confident Cook	Learning to Cook	Sticky Situation
Preparation	All ingredients are gathered; area is clean; tools are appropriate to the task.	Most ingredients are gathered and area is clean; one item or tool is missing.	Some ingredients and/or tools are missing; area is messy.	Ingredients and tools are missing and/or not appropriate to the task; area is messy.
Process	All steps to make the sandwich are followed and completed in a logical order.	Some steps to make the sandwich are missing or out of order.	Multiple steps to make the sandwich are missing or out of order.	Reflects no understanding of steps; steps are incomplete or not attempted.

---

5. Stevens and Levi, *Introduction to Rubrics*, 7.

Presentation	Sandwich is neat with even layers and is appetizing.	The layers are generally neat with minor mess.	The layers are messy/uneven; the sandwich is assembled but is not visually appealing.	Sandwich is overly messy and falling apart.

The above example illustrates the simplicity of rubric design. Educators can utilize a rubric to structure assessment for the most basic of tasks, even making a peanut butter and jelly sandwich. The task of making a peanut butter and jelly sandwich might be relatively simple, but the rubric brings greater clarity to the assignment and the educator's expectations.

Educators can also utilize these same steps for creating rubrics for the most complex and highest levels of learning. No matter the level, following the steps to create a rubric challenges the educator to think carefully about the assignment, find gaps in assignment instructions and expectations, and ultimately bring clarity to the assessment process.

Breaking Down the Process: Define Clear Criteria

Begin by *brainstorming and listing*. The first step in creating a rubric is to define clear criteria for the assignment. Begin by listing the key knowledge, attitudes, and skills to assess. This list should be broad and should capture any possible learning that class members should demonstrate. For example, in a research paper assignment, the educator might want to start with a list as broad as the following:

Structure	Creativity	Transitions
Flow	Style	Citation accuracy
Form	Tone	Conciseness
Depth of research	Grammar/mechanics	Clarity
Use of resources	Adherence to guidelines	Appropriate length
Organization	Argumentation	Analysis

At this stage, the focus is not on whether each of these criteria is redundant or even distinct. This list will contain overlapping ideas to refine and clarify later. The goal is to consider all of the knowledge, attitudes, and skills that the learner should demonstrate in completing the assignment. By brainstorming and listing, the educator is reflecting broadly on what

Assessing the Learning: The Rationale for Well-Designed Rubrics

learning he or she is aiming for the learner to achieve. Often in this phase, the listing itself can bring clarity to the scope and purpose of the assignment.

Next, *refine and simplify* the broad list to distinct criteria. Return to the course goals to find where to prioritize and focus the criteria. Returning to the example of a research paper assignment, the following questions might help refine and focus distinct criteria:

1. What level is the course (undergraduate, graduate, doctoral)?
2. What is the context of the course (how does this course fit within the program)?
3. What are the objectives for the course (is there a course objective that is specifically associated with this assignment)?

Answering these questions aligns the broad list of possible knowledge, attitudes, and skills with level, program, and course goals. The aim is to simplify the criteria and to emphasize the primary knowledge, attitudes, and skills that the assignment will assess.

This example assumes a doctoral-level, research-focused course on learning theories, with a course objective emphasizing thorough research and analysis of those theories. Those assumptions make it possible to synthesize the broader list to five distinct criteria:

1. Research and Analysis
2. Content and Argumentation
3. Organization and Structure
4. Clarity and Style
5. Mechanics and Formatting

These categories synthesize the broader list of criteria into distinct but meaningful categories. Because the rubric is for an assignment in a doctoral program for a research-focused course, the criteria emphasize the aspects of thorough research and scholarly writing. Although there are countless ways to refine these criteria, this list of five criteria offers clarity, simplicity, and alignment with the broader course and program contexts of the assignment.

Finally, *assign weight to each of the criteria* in the assignment. In this example, research is likely of primary importance given the significance of the research to both the course and the program. If so, it would be best to weight the research and analysis criterion more heavily than mechanics and formatting. Weighting the criteria highlights the most significant aspect(s) of an assignment. Learners can recognize easily the primary emphasis by looking at the weighting of the criteria:

Assignment:	Doctoral Research Paper			
Description:	Using recent scholarly sources, research, summarize, and critique two learning theories. Present your findings in a twelve-to-fifteen-page paper that follows proper Turabian format.			
Purpose:	To develop skill in researching, explaining, and critiquing a topic as well as in presenting findings clearly and accurately using good academic written style.			
	Performance Level	Performance Level	Performance Level	Performance Level
Research and Analysis (30%)				
Content and Argumentation (20%)				
Organization and Structure (20%)				
Clarity and Style (15%)				
Mechanics and Formatting (15%)				

Breaking Down the Process: Establish Learner-Friendly Performance Levels

Once the criteria are in place, create concise descriptive levels to describe the different performance levels for the criteria. The criteria define the categories (e.g., Clarity and Style), but the performance levels describe in greater detail what constitutes different levels of success in demonstrating these criteria.

The performance levels can describe the learner's level (novice to advanced) or the content's level (beginning to exceptional). Performance levels might follow the traditional A through F. More often though, they use descriptive language to categorize the levels. The aim is to provide clear and distinct labels for performance. Four distinct labels are typically sufficient to differentiate the levels of performance.

Again, the level of the assignment helps to guide the educator in choosing student-friendly language. In the example of the peanut butter and jelly assignment, the language was relaxed and approachable. It reflected the learner's level and the weight of the assignment. Returning to the example of the doctoral research paper, the performance levels still need to be clear and understandable, but they are likely to be more formal given the educational level:

Assignment:	Doctoral Research Paper			
Description:	Using recent scholarly sources, research, summarize, and critique two learning theories. Present your findings in a twelve-to-fifteen-page paper that follows proper Turabian format.			
Purpose:	To develop skill in researching, explaining, and critiquing a topic as well as in presenting findings clearly and accurately using good academic written style.			
	Advanced	Proficient	Developing	Beginning
Research and Analysis (30%)				
Content and Argumentation (20%)				
Organization and Structure (20%)				
Clarity and Style (15%)				
Mechanics and Formatting (15%)				

Breaking Down the Process: Develop Meaningful Descriptors

The final step for designing a rubric is to develop meaningful descriptors for each criterion under each of the performance levels. Descriptors allow the educator to flesh out the specific expectations in a way that provides actionable feedback for the learner. Although the performance levels and criteria broadly outline expectations, the descriptors detail these expectations. Through this step, the educator pulls back the curtain so that class members know exactly what the educator is seeking. The more detailed and objective the descriptors are, the more learners can self-assess and address deficiencies in their work.

The extent to which a rubric is effective often resides in the descriptors. Vague or unclear descriptors make it difficult for learners to know whether they have achieved a performance level. Specific and clear descriptors, however, give them the guidance that they need. Meaningful descriptors go beyond the primary objective of the assignment to identify how the educator identifies advanced research and analysis. The following example contrasts a vague descriptor with a meaningful descriptor.

Vague Descriptor	Research is thorough. Uses a sufficient number of resources. Resources used are scholarly and current. Analysis demonstrates critical thinking.
Meaningful Descriptor	Uses at least eight scholarly resources published in the last ten years. Includes at least three peer-reviewed journal articles. Analysis goes beyond summarizing the material to critique and identify both strengths and weaknesses of the material.

The meaningful descriptor includes the quantifiable expectation that names observable behaviors. From this descriptor, learners can understand the expectation for each level of performance. The following table adds meaningful descriptors to the rubric for a doctoral research paper:

Assignment:	Doctoral Research Paper			
Description:	Using recent scholarly sources, research, summarize, and critique two learning theories. Present your findings in a twelve-to-fifteen-page paper that follows proper Turabian format.			
Purpose:	To develop skill in researching, explaining, and critiquing a topic as well as in presenting findings clearly and accurately using good academic written style.			
	Advanced	Proficient	Developing	Beginning
Research and Analysis (30%)	Utilizes at least eight scholarly resources published in the last ten years; includes at least three peer-reviewed journal articles. Analysis goes beyond summarizing the material to critique both strengths and weaknesses of the material. (30–23 pts.)	Utilizes at least six scholarly resources published in the last fifteen years; includes at least two peer-reviewed journal articles. Analysis primarily summarizes; includes some critique. (22–15 pts.)	Utilizes at least four scholarly resources published in the last twenty years; includes at least one peer-reviewed journal article. Analysis primarily summarizes; includes minimal critique. (14–7 pts.)	Utilizes at least two scholarly resources published in the last twenty years; includes no peer-reviewed journal articles. Analysis primarily summarizes; includes no critique. (6–0 pts.)

Content and Argumentation (20%)	Longer than twelve pages. Outlines two learning theories thoroughly. Explains the history, proponents, and major tenets of each theory in detail. Makes clear connection between research findings and central argument. (20–15 pts.)	At least twelve pages. Outlines two learning theories adequately. Explains the history, proponents, and major tenets of each theory briefly. Makes some connection between research findings and central argument. (14–10 pts.)	At least ten pages. Outlines two learning theories briefly. Omits explanation of one or more elements of either or both theories. Makes minimal connection between research findings and central argument. (9–5 pts.)	Fewer than ten pages. Outlines one learning theory. Presentation lacks explanation. Makes no connection between research findings and central argument. (4–0 pts.)
Organization and Structure (20%)	Organizes ideas logically; sections build on what precedes; good transitions lead to good flow. (20–15 pts.)	Organizes ideas somewhat logically; includes some transitions; pays little attention to flow. (14–10 pts.)	Lacks logical organization; includes very few transitions; flow of argument is hard to follow. (9–5 pts.)	Work is disorganized; includes no transitions; flow is incoherent. (4–0 pts.)
Clarity and Style (15%)	Writes in third person and active voice; uses no contractions. Style is consistently objective. (15–12 pts.)	Occasionally writes in first person or passive voice; uses some contractions. Style is mostly objective. (11–8 pts.)	Frequently writes in first person and passive voice; uses frequent contractions. Style lacks objectivity. (7–4 pts.)	Writes entirely in first person and passive voice; uses multiple contractions. Style is pejorative. (3–0 pts.)

Mechanics and Formatting (15%)	Virtually no errors in grammar, spelling, citation, and Turabian formatting. Follows all assignment guidelines. (15–12 pts.)	Fewer than five errors in grammar, spelling, citation, and Turabian formatting. Follows most assignment guidelines. (11–8 pts.)	More than five errors in grammar, spelling, citation, and Turabian formatting. Follows some assignment guidelines. (7–4 pts.)	More that ten errors in grammar, spelling, citation, and Turabian formatting. Follows few assignment guidelines. (3–0 pts.)

Also included in the performance descriptors above are the specific points associated with each performance level. Including the point levels allows for easy scoring when grading. The educator can identify overall where the learner's performance level is and then has some additional flexibility to award the full points for that performance level or a lower amount based on how fully the learner met that level. Point levels also help class members recognize the impact of each level on their final grade.

Best Practices for Using Rubrics

As with any educational practice, educators achieve various levels of success in utilizing rubrics depending on their application. A rubric is primarily an assessment tool to evaluate work on assignments, but the educator can also use the rubric as a communication tool. When educators share rubrics as part of the assignment brief, students have greater clarity about assignment expectations.

Understanding that rubrics serve as a way to communicate assignment expectations, the educator uses *clear and accessible language*. The goal is for class members to read the rubric and understand more accurately what behavior and skills they should demonstrate in their work. Rather than vague, broad terms, educators write rubrics to reinforce learning. They want students to read the rubric and have a clear and accurate picture of how to assess their work.

Whenever possible, the educator makes rubrics *specific to individual assignments*. Although developing rubrics can be time-consuming, a best practice is to revise rubrics regularly and tailor them to specific assignments. Although initially a general rubric for a research paper or discussion board is sufficient, the more that the educator uses the rubric not only for grading but as a learning tool, the more customized rubrics enhance the learning and the assessment.

The educator also makes sure that the performance levels are distinct *with concrete descriptors* that learners can easily use to measure their work. Rubrics should include precise measures for the different levels of performance. The best rubrics are so concrete and objective that virtually anyone can use them and assign the same grade.

The best use of rubrics is to *share them early* and *provide guidance* on their use. Educators can be explicit as to the standards and expectations of the assignment by sharing the rubric as part of assignment instructions or even by including it as soon as they publish their syllabus. Making the rubric accessible, however, does not guarantee that class members will use the tool to guide their learning. The educator should give careful thought as to how best to involve learners in the assessment process.

Involving Learners in the Assessment Process

Learners might also have a wide array of prior experience with using rubrics, depending on their educational backgrounds. Colleges and universities only began to utilize rubrics widely in the last twenty years. Even if learners have encountered rubrics in past educational experiences, it is possible, if not probable, that they viewed rubrics primarily as a helpful tool for the educator to streamline grading. Although rubrics certainly serve that purpose, for the learning-centered educator, the rubric can be an indispensable tool in facilitating learning. Given the limited and only recent use of rubrics, the educator should not assume that class members know how to use the rubric effectively. Instead, they can show students how to get the most value from the rubric by involving them in the assessment process.

The wise educator will take time to find meaningful ways to incorporate rubrics into instruction, even to the point of explaining the use of each rubric and having class members practice using the rubric in peer or self-assessment. Although they often view rubrics solely as grading tools for summative assessment, educators might find ways to utilize them in *formative assessment*. In the example of the research paper, class members might assess each other's work in peer review. The rubric then becomes a tool for guiding peer review and prepares them for the summative assessment.

Educators might also use rubrics to guide learners in a reflective practice for *self-assessment*. By incorporating the use of the rubric into a self-assessment requirement, the educator involves learners in applying the rubric to their own work. Self-assessment is an excellent way to learn how effectively the educator has applied the best practices above. As learners attempt to utilize the rubric in self-assessment, the educator can gain real-time feedback into the accessibility and objectivity of the rubric. If class members attempt to use the rubric as a self-assessment and are not able to employ the rubric effectively, then there likely are some weaknesses in the rubric design.

Educators might consider a more radical approach to involving learners in the assessment process by *co-creating rubrics*. As simple as the steps to developing a rubric are, class members can participate in developing an assignment rubric. As with any learning, the educator remains the guide, directing learners to the necessary outcomes. By taking the time to involve class members in creating a rubric, the educator fosters ownership and understanding. By guiding them in developing a rubric, the educator encourages learner buy-in through transparency and collaboration.

Sample Rubrics

The following examples serve as illustrations of best practices in rubrics as well as possible templates for use with similar assignments. Note that each rubric includes a column to record the score for each criterion as well as a total score for the assignment. The rubrics for the more complex assignments also include space for comments and/or notes.

Assignment:	Online Discussion			
Description:	Participate in an online discussion forum by posting an initial post responding to a provided prompt (minimum of 500 words by Wednesday at midnight) and responding to at least two classmates (minimum of 250 words each by Saturday at midnight).			
Purpose:	To deepen your understanding of course concepts through meaningful dialogue with your classmates.			
	Exemplary (8–10)	Capable (5–7)	Needs Work (1–4)	Score
Engagement with the Prompt	Engages the prompt thoughtfully; demonstrates critical thinking and analysis; goes beyond summarizing the course material; meets the required word minimum (500 words).	Engages the prompt appropriately; demonstrates some critical thinking and analysis; mostly summarizes the course material; meets the required word minimum (500 words).	Engages the prompt indifferently; demonstrates little critical thinking and analysis; summarizes the course material; does not meet the required word minimum (500 words).	
Thoughtfulness of Response to Others	Responds to classmates' posts thoughtfully; asks meaningful questions and deepens the conversation through specific observations; uses an appropriate and respectful tone; meets the required word minimum (250 words).	Responds to classmates' posts appropriately; asks some meaningful questions and makes some specific observations; mostly uses an appropriate and respectful tone; meets the required word minimum (250 words).	Responds to classmates' posts indifferently; does not demonstrate a careful reading of classmates' posts; uses a disrespectful or argumentative tone; falls significantly short of required word minimum (250 words).	
Timeliness	Initial post submitted by Wednesday at midnight; response posts by Saturday at midnight.	Initial post submitted by Wednesday at midnight; response posts submitted late.	Initial post submitted late; response posts late or not submitted.	

Grammar and Mechanics	Few to no issues with grammar or sentence mechanics.	Three of more issues with grammar or sentence mechanics.	Five or more issues with grammar or sentence mechanics.	
			Total Score	/40

Assignment: Oral Presentation
Description: Deliver a five-to-seven-minute oral presentation on an assigned topic, incorporating at least one visual aid.
Purpose: To practice communicating effectively in a group setting.

	Excellent	Proficient	Developing	Beginning	Score
Content and Organization (40%)	Shows strong understanding of the content; explains content thoroughly; uses clear structure; supports ideas with appropriate evidence. (40–37)	Shows solid understanding of the content; explains content adequately; has some structure; supports ideas with some evidence. (36–33)	Shows some understanding of the content; explains content poorly; structure is hard to follow; supports ideas with little evidence. (32–29)	Shows little understanding of the content; explains content incoherently; structure is confusing; does not support ideas. (28–0)	
Audience Engagement and Delivery (25%)	Engaging delivery; excellent pacing; consistent eye contact; intentional gestures. (25–23)	Clear delivery; appropriate pacing; good eye contact; unplanned gestures. (22–20)	Uncertain delivery; uneven pacing; limited eye contact; few gestures. (19–17)	Garbled delivery; rushed or slow pacing; no eye contact; no gestures. (16–0)	

Visuals (15%)	Visuals enhance the presentation, making the material clearer and more engaging. (15–14)	Visuals are clear and complement the presentation. (13–12)	Visuals are unclear and do not add to the presentation. (11–10)	Visuals are missing or not relevant to the presentation. (9–0)	
Time Management (10%)	Covers all of the material; falls within the time frame (5–7 minutes); no rushing or dragging. (10)	Covers most of the material; falls within the time frame (5–7); minimal rushing or dragging. (9)	Covers most of the material; falls within 1–2 minutes of the time frame (5–7 minutes); some rushing or dragging. (8)	Omits part of the material; is 2 or more minutes over or under the time frame (5–7 minutes); consistent rushing or dragging. (7–0)	
Grammar and Mechanics (10%)	Few or no filler words or poor word choices; no incomplete sentences; mechanics add polish and professionalism to the content. (10)	More than three filler words or poor word choices; one or two incomplete sentences; mechanics do not detract from the content. (9)	More than five filler words or poor word choices; several incomplete sentences; mechanics detract somewhat from the content. (8)	Numerous filler words and/or poor word choices; multiple incomplete sentences; mechanics detract significantly from the content. (7–0)	
Comments/Notes:				Total Score	

Assignment:	Group Project on Spiritual Disciplines
Description:	In a group of four to five students, research a spiritual discipline assigned by the instructor. As a group, design and implement a plan for how to practice the discipline over a three-week period. Reflect and report on that experience by preparing a ten-to-fifteen-minute group presentation that includes biblical teachings on the discipline, past and present practice in the church, and recommendations for how to incorporate the discipline based on the group's experience.
Purpose:	To develop a deeper understanding of a spiritual discipline through research, practical application, and reflection while strengthening collaboration and presentation skills.

	Outstanding	Strong	Basic	Lacking	Score
Biblical and Historical Context (20%)	Showed strong understanding of the biblical and historical contexts; explained contexts thoroughly. (20–19)	Showed solid understanding of the biblical and historical contexts; explained contexts adequately. (18–17)	Showed some understanding of the biblical and historical contexts; explained contexts poorly. (16–15)	Showed little understanding of the biblical and historical contexts; did not explain contexts. (14–0)	
Group Plan and Reflection (30%)	Emphasized biblical teaching; explained past and present practice thoroughly; reflected thoughtfully on implementation by the group. (30–28)	Included biblical teaching; explained past and present practice; reflected on implementation by the group. (27–25)	Mentioned biblical teaching; explained past and present practice briefly; reflected superficially on implementation by the group. (24–22)	Omitted biblical teaching; included no explanation of past and present practice; included little reflection on implementation by the group. (21–0)	

Presentation Effectiveness (20%)	Presented material in an engaging manner; used visuals well; stayed within the time frame. (20–19)	Presented material clearly; used an appropriate number of visuals; stayed within the time frame. (18–17)	Presented material in an informal manner; used a few visuals; stayed within 1–2 minutes of the time frame. (16–15)	Presented material in a sloppy manner; used no visuals; exceeded or fell short of the time frame by 2 or more minutes. (14–0)	
Group Collaboration (20%)	Members of the group collaborated actively and willingly. (20–19)	Members of the group collaborated equally and well. (18–17)	Some members of the group collaborated fully; others did not. (16–15)	Members of the group worked individually and did not collaborate. (14–0)	
Clarity and Mechanics (10%)	Oral delivery was polished; mechanics added professionalism to the delivery. (10)	Oral delivery was clear; mechanics did not detract from the delivery. (9)	Oral delivery was uncertain; mechanics detracted somewhat from the delivery. (8)	Oral delivery was poor; mechanics detracted significantly from the delivery. (7–0)	
Comments/Notes:				Total Score	

Assignment:	Reflective Essay		
Description:	After completing the assigned reading, reflect on your own experience as it relates to the reading. Write a 500-word essay reflecting on insights from the reading and how you plan to apply those insights in your personal or professional context.		
Purpose:	To deepen understanding of the reading through personal reflection and practical application.		
	Full Marks (5 pts)	No Marks (0 pts)	Score
Assignment Length	Meets the required number of words (≥ 500).	Falls well below the required number of words ($200 \geq$).	
Mechanics and Clarity	Writes clearly and precisely with few stylistic errors.	Writes unclearly and poorly with multiple stylistic errors.	
Evidence of Reading	Makes clear and specific connections to the assigned reading.	Makes no connections to the assigned reading.	
Personal Reflection	Identifies at least two personal insights from the assigned reading.	Identifies no personal insights from the assigned reading.	
Plan for Application	Describes specific and detailed action steps to take.	Describes no action steps to take.	
		Total Score	/25

Conclusion

Rubrics support the work of both educators and the learners by bringing clarity to the educational process. They reinforce learning goals and increase transparency. They remove the guesswork from assessments and keep the focus on learning. They provide means of summative assessment, formative assessment, and learner self-assessment. They communicate expectations and provide actionable feedback. They foster trust, fairness, and confidence.

Rubrics are an integral part of the learning process. They can be simple or complex. They can assess a variety of assignments and can use a variety of approaches. Designing them involves a simple, three-step process that can apply to any assignment, but learning-centered educators are always adopting and refining their rubrics in order to serve learners more effectively. With rubrics, the educator reinforces learning, pulls back the curtain on assessment, and guides the learner in the educational process.

Food for Thought
How do rubrics currently support student learning in your courses?
What is one assignment or assessment where a well-designed rubric could improve clarity and fairness?
Do your rubrics clearly communicate expectations and provide actionable feedback for learners?
When might you dedicate time to create or refine a rubric using the principles outlined in this chapter?

6

Plan the Learning: The Blueprint for a Transformational Lesson

Chapter Preview
A learning-centered approach to lesson planning distributes learning across three learning spaces.
Crafting a memorable big idea for the lesson and establishing an overarching lesson goal helps keep learning on track.
A transformational lesson plan addresses all three levels of learning and all three domains of learning.

THE GOAL IS LEARNING, and a learning-centered lesson facilitates interactive learning and aims to transform the entire learner. The starting point for planning such a lesson is adopting a model that addresses all three levels of learning. That model goes beyond traditional and flipped models of lesson planning to make use of three distinct learning spaces.

The Traditional Model

Traditional lesson planning follows a model in which learners gain their initial orientation to new material in the classroom, most commonly by taking notes while an instructor lectures. Learners might have read about the concepts before coming to class, but the instructor is the expert who makes certain that they understand what was important in their reading. As a "sage on the stage," the instructor dispenses content actively, and learners receive it passively. After class, the instructor is absent, and learners are on their own to appropriate and apply the content. The in-class space focuses on lower-level learning, while the post-class space focuses on higher-level learning. The model tends to align with the standard workload allocation of one hour in class and two hours out of class for each credit hour of study. Schematically, the following table captures the relationships between learning spaces, educator and student roles, and levels of learning in the traditional model:

Learning Space	Educator Role	Learner Role	Learning Level
In-Class	Present content	Acquire content	Level 1
Post-Class	—	Apply content	Level 2

Talbert notes four crucial issues with the traditional model:[1]

1. The traditional model creates an inverse relationship between cognitive difficulty of student work and student access to support.
2. The traditional model takes time away from guided exploration of deeper learning.
3. The traditional model does not promote self-regulated learning behaviors.
4. The traditional model creates undesirable intellectual dependencies of students on instructors.

The Flipped Model

Just as educators have suggested alternatives to the traditional approach to course design, they have also suggested alternatives to the traditional model of lesson planning. One of those alternatives is commonly labeled "flipped learning." Talbert defines flipped learning as "a pedagogical approach in which first contact with new concepts moves from the group learning space to the individual learning space . . . and the resulting group space

---

1. Talbert, *Flipped Learning*, 5.

is transformed into a[n] . . . interactive learning environment where the educator guides students as . . . they engage the subject matter."[2]

The model is "flipped" because it reverses the contexts of learning and the roles of educator and learner. Learners gain their initial orientation to new content outside the classroom, while the educator becomes a "guide on the side" who facilitates application of the content during class sessions. Learners are active learners, and the educator is present as a resource who answers questions and coaches learners as they work. The pre-class space focuses on lower-level learning, while the in-class space focuses on higher-level learning. Schematically, the following table captures the relationships between learning spaces, educator and learner roles, and levels of learning in the flipped model:

Learning Space	Educator Role	Learner Role	Learning Level
Pre-Class	Prepare content	Acquire content	Level 1
In-Class	Facilitate learning	Apply content	Level 2

Talbert notes that the flipped model addresses each of the four issues he has raised in regard to the traditional model:[3]

1. The relation between cognitive difficulty and access to support is direct.
2. The in-class space is open for the instructor to design activities that explore deeper learning.
3. Students must practice self-regulated learning behaviors on a regular basis.
4. Shifting the instructor's role to coach/consultant fosters a more "grown-up" relationship with students.

The ways in which educators prepare content for the pre-class space and learners acquire that content vary. Reading and videos are the most common resources. Educators might create their own videos, or they might use existing online videos. Talbert suggests a mix of media—video, text, audio, computer simulations, computer games—as well as giving learners a

---

2. Talbert, *Flipped Learning*, 20. As will become clearer in the next section, what Talbert labels as the "individual space" is perhaps better considered the "pre-class space," and what he labels as the "group space" is perhaps better considered the "in-class space."

3. Talbert, *Flipped Learning*, 8.

choice from a playlist.[4] The key is to give learners the best resources possible to orient them to the information that they will need to be ready to engage higher-level goals in the in-class space.

Subsequent sections of this chapter will discuss the details of planning the pre-class and in-class spaces, but the flipped model also recognizes that there are often tasks related to lesson goals that require more time than is available during the in-class space. Talbert discusses "post-group activities" briefly, but it is almost an afterthought, and he acknowledges that those activities differ little from the activities of the traditional post-class space.[5] A model that intentionally uses all three spaces as part of lesson planning, though, has the potential to address all three levels of learning.

The Stair-Step Model

Chapter 3 proposed a three-level multitiered approach to course design. The following table focuses on the three domains of content, character, and competence from that proposal:

	Content	Character	Competence
Level 1	Comprehend	Receive	Reproduce
Level 2	Analyze	Respond	Reorganize
Level 3	Create	Value	Innovate

Similarly, a balanced, learning-centered approach to lesson planning will seek to include all three levels and will include goals that address all three domains. A model that uses all three learning spaces seems particularly well-suited to address different levels of learning in all three domains. Educationally, if level 1 learning lays the foundation on which higher levels build, the result is a three-tiered stair-step model that uses all three spaces:

		Level 3 Learning	Post-Class Space
	Level 2 Learning		In-Class Space
Level 1 Learning			Pre-class Space

The stair-step model is similar to the discussion in chapter 3 of units within a course that build upon one another and increase in complexity. The implementation, though, is in lesson planning rather than in course design.

---

4. Talbert, *Flipped Learning*, 141.
5. Talbert, *Flipped Learning*, 144.

It combines the three spaces of the traditional and flipped models, retains the educator and learner roles of the flipped model, and raises the level of post-space learning beyond the traditional model. Schematically, the following table captures the relationships between learning spaces, educator and learner roles, and levels of learning in the stair-step model:

Learning Space	Educator Role	Learner Role	Learning Level
Pre-Class	Prepare content	Acquire content	Level 1
In-Class	Facilitate learning	Apply content	Level 2
Post-Class	—	Appropriate content	Level 3

In the traditional model, the standard workload allocation of one hour in class and two hours out of class for each credit hour would equate to three hours in class and six hours after class for a three-credit course. In the flipped model, the workload allocation would equate to six hours before class and three hours in class. The stair-step model allocates workload to three hours in each space—pre-class, in-class, and post-class.

Planning a Lesson That Uses the Stair-Step Model

Planning a lesson that uses the stair-step model follows a six-step process that begins at the "big idea" level:

1. Craft a big idea.
2. Establish an overarching lesson goal.
3. Develop ABOs for the lesson.
4. Sort the ABOs by level of learning.
5. Assign the ABOs to the three learning spaces.
6. Design learning tasks to achieve the ABOs in each space.

The following template serves as a guide through the lesson planning process. Note that it includes intentional planning for each of the three learning spaces:

Lesson Plan Template	
Lesson Overview	
Course	
Instructor	
Topic	
Lesson Big Idea	
Lesson Goal	
Lesson ABOs and Learning Spaces	
Pre-Class Space	
In-Class Space	
Post-Class Space	
Pre-Class Learning Space	
Overview	
Goal(s)	
Resource(s)	
Task(s)	
Assessment	
In-Class Learning Space	
Overview	
Goal(s)	
Resource(s)	
Opening Stage Task	
Middle Stage Tasks	
Closing Stage Task	
Assessment	
Post-Class Learning Space	
Overview	
Goal(s)	
Resource(s)	
Task(s)	
Assessment	

The first step is to *craft a big idea* for the lesson. The big idea is a single, concise sentence that captures both the topic and the focus of the lesson. As a sentence, it consists of a subject and a complement. The subject identifies the topic (What are we studying?), and the complement identifies the focus (What are we learning about what we are studying?) This step takes work, because the big idea must be both concise enough to be memorable and precise enough to keep the lesson on track.

Having a clearly articulated big idea benefits the educator, the lesson, and the learners. It keeps the educator focused on the topic. It keeps the lesson focused on the target. It keeps the learners focused on the task. Here are possible big ideas for lessons on three different topics:

Lesson Big Idea
Topic: Word Study (Hermeneutics)
Big Idea: Lexical analysis gives a word precision and texture.
Topic: Doctrine of Inspiration (Theology)
Big Idea: Inspired Scripture is authoritative in everything it teaches and touches.
Topic: Expository Sermon (Homiletics)
Big Idea: Expository preaching explains and expounds the truth of Scripture.

The second step is to *establish an overarching goal* for the lesson. Because a learning-centered lesson will aim to go beyond simply communicating information, the lesson goal should include both a content element and either a character element or a competence element. Because the lesson goal defines what learners will have done by the end of the lesson, it will begin with the phrase "By the end of this lesson." The basic template for an overarching lesson goal, therefore, is:

> By the end of this lesson, learners will have . . . (Content), and will have . . . (Character/Competence).

Writing an overarching goal for the entire lesson gives the lesson focus, continuity, and a basis for assessing learning. Here are possible overarching goals for lessons on the three topics above:

Lesson Goal
Word Study (Hermeneutics)
By the end of this lesson, learners will have reviewed essential components of lexical analysis, and will have practiced a systematic method for doing a word study.
Doctrine of Inspiration (Theology)
By the end of this lesson, learners will have reviewed essential aspects of the doctrine of inspiration, and will have explored the implications of the doctrine for the interpretation of Scripture.
Expository Preaching (Homiletics)
By the end of this lesson, learners will have reviewed essential aspects of expository preaching, and will have designed a sermon that accurately communicates the truth of a Scripture passage.

The third step is to *develop ABOs* for the lesson. Chapter 3 introduced Vella's approach of writing goals as achievement-based objectives (ABOs) rather than ability-based objectives. In that chapter, the approach applied to the goals for a course. In this chapter, it applies to the goals for a lesson. The lesson ABOs describe what students will have done as the result of engaging the knowledge and skills that are part of the lesson.

The initial list of ABOs for the lesson should address the elements of the lesson that learners must master in order for them to achieve the overarching lesson goal. A comprehensive, well-written list of ABOs will address all three levels of learning and as many domains of learning as possible. There is no need to sort them in this step, though, since sorting is the task of the next step. Here are possible ABOs for a lesson on the doctrine of inspiration in a theology course:

Lesson ABOs
By the end of the lesson, class members will have • Distinguished inspiration from revelation and illumination. • Articulated a biblically-informed definition of the doctrine of inspiration. • Categorized the properties of Scripture that result from inspiration. • Explored the implications of the doctrine of inspiration for dealing with apparent discrepancies in Scripture. • Reviewed the biblical support for the doctrine of inspiration. • Described the process by which the Holy Spirit used the human authors to record the message of Scripture. • Explained the concept of verbal plenary inspiration.

The fourth step is to *sort the ABOs* by level of learning. Chapter 3 included a matrix of verbs that can serve as starting points for a list of lesson ABOs that can address a variety of levels and domains of learning. It might be necessary to rewrite some of the initial ABOs in order to align them with the three levels of learning. Here is a sorted list for the lesson on the doctrine of inspiration in a theology course:

	Lesson ABOs Sorted by Level of Learning
Level 1 ABOs	• Reviewed the biblical support for the doctrine of inspiration. • Described the process by which the Holy Spirit used the human authors to record the message of Scripture. • Articulated a biblically-informed definition of the doctrine of inspiration.
Level 2 ABOs	• Explained the concept of verbal plenary inspiration. • Categorized the properties of Scripture that result from inspiration. • Distinguished inspiration from revelation and illumination.
Level 3 ABOs	• Explored the implications of the doctrine of inspiration for dealing with apparent discrepancies in Scripture.

The fifth step is to *assign the ABOs* to the three learning spaces. If the sorted ABOs address all three levels of learning, they align naturally with the stair-step model of lesson planning and allow the ABOs to build upon one another and increase in complexity as the lesson moves though the three learning spaces. Assigning them to the learning spaces is relatively simple. Here are the results for a lesson on the doctrine of inspiration in a theology course:

	Lesson ABOs and Learning Spaces
Pre-Class Space	• Reviewed the biblical support for the doctrine of inspiration. • Articulated a biblically-informed definition of the doctrine of inspiration. • Described the process by which the Holy Spirit used the human authors to record the message of Scripture.
In-Class Space	• Explained the concept of verbal plenary inspiration. • Categorized the properties of Scripture that result from inspiration. • Distinguished inspiration from revelation and illumination.

Post-Class Space	• Explored the implications of the doctrine of inspiration for dealing with apparent discrepancies in Scripture.

The sixth step is to *design learning tasks* for each learning space. Chapter 7 will explore learning tasks in detail. The remainder of this chapter will suggest examples of possible learning tasks for each of the three spaces of a lesson on the doctrine of inspiration in a theology course.

For the pre-class space, Talbert suggests a "guided practice" model that includes five elements.[6] A modified version of those five elements provides a helpful pattern for designing each of the three learning spaces:

1. Overview—A brief description that introduces the learning and connects it to other aspects of the course and/or lesson.
2. Goal(s)—A list of the ABOs that the learners will have achieved by engaging in the learning tasks.
3. Resource(s)—A list of texts, videos, and/or other resources that the learners will use as they engage in the learning tasks.
4. Task(s)—A description of the learning tasks that the learners will use to achieve the ABOs.
5. Assessment—A description of the deliverables the learners will submit as evidence that they have completed the learning tasks.

The following sections will use those five elements to outline plans for each of the three learning spaces:

Planning the Pre-Class Space

The pre-class space focuses on level-one ABOs, requires basic resources for completing the tasks, assigns tasks that learners can complete independently, and uses low-stakes writing assignments as a means of assessment.[7] The following example applies the five-element pattern to the pre-class learning space:

---

6. Talbert, *Flipped Learning*, 134–39.

7. For the concept of low-stakes writing assignments, see McKeachie and Svinicki, *Teaching Tips*, 214–17.

	Pre-Class Learning Space
Overview	A narrated PowerPoint will explain the relationship between revelation and inspiration, offer a definition of inspiration, and suggest Scripture passages to study in support of the doctrine.
Goal(s)	After you have completed the assigned reading and tasks, you will have • Reviewed the biblical support for the doctrine of inspiration. • Articulated a biblically-informed definition of the doctrine of inspiration. • Described the process by which the Holy Spirit used the human authors to record the message of Scripture.
Resource(s)	Reading: Pache, *The Inspiration and Authority of Scripture*, chapters 5–9.
Task(s)	As you read, take notes that you can use to answer the following questions: What do two key Scripture passages teach about the doctrine of inspiration? How would you define inspiration for a new Christian? How would you explain the process of inspiration to a new Christian?
Assessment	Write one-paragraph answers to the three questions and post them to Assignment #1 on the Canvas course site **at least one hour before the class session begins**.

Using low-stakes writing assignments as the means of assessment in the pre-class space accomplishes two purposes. First, it gives learners the opportunity to articulate their initial understanding of a topic. Second, it addresses the frequently-raised concern, "What if students skip the pre-class tasks?" In order to keep the stakes low, it is usually best to grade assignments as complete or incomplete. In order to give the assignments some weight, though, it is best to assign a percentage of the overall course grade to completion of pre-class assignments.

Planning the In-Class Space

It is best to plan the in-class space around three stages—opening stage, middle stage, and closing stage.[8] The opening stage composes 10–20 percent of the class time and connects what learners have already explored in the pre-class space to what they are about to explore in the in-class space. The

8. Talbert, *Flipped Learning*, 126–29.

learning task for the opening stage might take the form of listening to a brief lecture, viewing a brief video, taking a brief quiz, or discussing a thought-provoking question. The objectives in the opening stage are to pique the learners' interest and begin moving them toward the learning task(s) of the middle stage.

The middle stage composes 60–80 percent of the class time and focuses on the learning tasks that allow learners to achieve the level-two ABOs of the lesson. The only limit on the learning tasks is the educator's creativity. They could be anything that challenges learners to engage the material for themselves, whether group discussions, mini-debates, problem-solving exercises, or other tasks. Chapter 7 will discuss learning tasks in detail. The educator provides the resources and the structure, and then acts as a coach while class members actively engage in the learning tasks together. Vella's parts of a learning task are a helpful model: *input* (introduce the new content), *implementation* (use the new content), and *integration* (apply the new content).[9]

The closing stage composes 10–20 percent of the class time and focuses on summarizing, synthesizing, and reflecting. Talbert suggests that the closing stage can raise issues such as lessons learned, difficulties encountered, and plans for personal application.[10] The closing stage of the in-class space is the connect-the-dots portion of the lesson.

The following example presupposes a single three-hour class period. The middle stage consists of six learning tasks that could also serve three one-hour class periods if the course schedule requires them (e.g., Monday-Wednesday-Friday with one-hour class periods on each day). The learning modalities are an online audience response application, mini-lectures (five to ten minutes each), small group discussions, and large group summaries. The opening and closing stages mirror one another and give class members an opportunity to self-evaluate their progress toward achieving the three lesson goals.

In-Class Learning Space	
Overview	Mini-lectures and small group discussions will help you refine your understanding of the details of the doctrine of inspiration.

---

9. Vella, *On Teaching and Learning*, 62–66. Input, implementation, and integration are the second, third, and fourth parts of her model. The first is inductive work.

10. Talbert, *Flipped Learning*, 129.

Goal(s)	After you have completed the assigned learning tasks, you will have • Explained the concept of verbal plenary inspiration. • Categorized the properties of Scripture that result from inspiration. • Distinguished inspiration from revelation and illumination.
Resource(s)	Fill-in-the-blank handouts: Theories of Inspiration Properties Resulting from Inspiration Revelation, Inspiration, and Illumination
Opening Stage Task	Learning Task #1: Using Poll Everywhere, take a brief "Inspiration IQ Quiz" that covers different theories of inspiration and properties that result from inspiration and discuss the results.
Middle Stage Tasks	Learning Task #2: Take notes on a mini-lecture over different theories of inspiration. Learning Task #3: Pair-Square-Share • In pairs, discuss the implications of the doctrine of verbal plenary inspiration. • With another pair, compare notes. • Share your group's findings with the rest of the class. Learning Task #4: Take notes on a mini-lecture over the properties that result from inspiration. Learning Task #5: Pair-Square-Share • In pairs, discuss the implications of each property that results from inspiration. • With another pair, compare notes. • Share your group's findings with the rest of the class. Learning Task #6: Take notes on a mini-lecture that defines revelation, inspiration, and illumination. Learning Task #7: Pair-Square-Share • In pairs, complete a table comparing revelation, inspiration, and illumination. • With another pair, compare notes. • Share your group's findings with the rest of the class.
Closing Stage Task	Learning Task #8: Using Poll Everywhere, retake the "Inspiration IQ Quiz" and discuss the results.
Assessment	Submit completed handouts for the instructor to review and return.

Planning the Post-Class Space

The post-class space returns to tasks that learners complete independently, requires resources for completing the tasks, and focuses on the highest-level ABOs in the lesson. The following example applies the overview-goals-resources-tasks-assessment pattern to the post-class learning space:

	Post-Class Learning Space
Overview	Assigned reading will prepare you to address apparent discrepancies in Scripture under a commitment to the verbal plenary inspiration of the Bible.
Goal(s)	After you have completed the assigned reading and tasks, you will have • Explored the implications of the doctrine of inspiration for dealing with apparent discrepancies in Scripture.
Resource(s)	Reading: McQuilkin, *Understanding and Applying the Bible*, chapter 17.
Task(s)	As you read, identify and record presuppositions and principles that align with the doctrine of verbal plenary inspiration of the Bible to use in dealing with apparent discrepancies in Scripture.
Assessment	For each set of passages below, (1) identify the apparent discrepancy(s), (2) state the principle(s) that apply, and (3) provide a possible solution to the apparent discrepancy(s). Write your answers in paragraph form with a cover page and submit them to Assignment #3 on the Canvas course site **by the day and time stated in the syllabus.** Matthew 15:39; Mark 8:10 Ephesians 4:10; Psalm 68:18 Matthew 2:15; Hosea 11:1 Matthew 20:29–34; Mark 10:46–52; Luke 18:35–43

Conclusion

A learning-centered approach to lesson planning revolves around a central lesson goal, addresses all three levels of learning and all three domains of learning, distributes learning across three learning spaces, and uses learning tasks to help learners achieve lesson ABOs. The process of lesson planning moves from crafting a big idea to establishing an overarching goal to developing, sorting, and distributing ABOs to designing learning tasks for pre-class, in-class, and post-class learning spaces. That process requires intentional thought and allows for considerable creativity. The payoff is a lesson that engages learners, facilitates learning, and has the potential to change the lives of the learners. The following pages set out an example of a completed lesson plan template.

Food for Thought
What are possible big ideas and lesson goals for some of the lessons that you lead on a regular basis?
How might you adjust some of your current lessons to address different levels and domains of learning?
What is one lesson you lead that might lend itself to a stair-step model of lesson planning?
What are some active learning tasks that you could use during a class period of one of the courses you teach?

Lesson Plan for a Class on the Doctrine of Inspiration in a Course on Theology and Ethics

\multicolumn{2}{c}{Lesson Plan Template}	
\multicolumn{2}{c}{**Lesson Overview**}	
Course	Theology and Ethics 1
Instructor	Dr. Theophilus Smith
Topic	Doctrine of Inspiration
Lesson Big Idea	Inspired Scripture is authoritative in everything it teaches and touches.
Lesson Goal	By the end of this lesson, learners will have reviewed essential aspects of the doctrine of inspiration and will have explored the implications of the doctrine for the interpretation of Scripture.
\multicolumn{2}{c}{**Lesson ABOs and Learning Spaces**}	
Pre-Class Space	After you have completed the assigned reading and tasks, you will have • Reviewed the biblical support for the doctrine of inspiration. • Described the process by which the Holy Spirit used the human authors to record the message of Scripture. • Articulated a biblically-informed definition of the doctrine of inspiration.
In-Class Space	After you have completed the assigned reading and tasks, you will have • Explained the concept of verbal plenary inspiration. • Categorized the properties of Scripture that result from inspiration. • Distinguished inspiration from revelation and illumination.
Post-Class Space	After you have completed the assigned learning tasks, you will have • Explored the implications of the doctrine of inspiration for dealing with apparent discrepancies in Scripture.

	Pre-Class Learning Space
Overview	A narrated PowerPoint will explain the relationship between revelation and inspiration, offer a definition of inspiration, and suggest Scripture passages to study in support of the doctrine.
Goal(s)	After you have completed the assigned reading and tasks, you will have • Reviewed the biblical support for the doctrine of inspiration. • Articulated a biblically-informed definition of the doctrine of inspiration. • Described the process by which the Holy Spirit used the human authors to record the message of Scripture.
Resource(s)	Reading: Pache, *The Inspiration and Authority of Scripture*, chapters 5–9.
Task(s)	As you read, take notes that you can use to answer the following questions: What do two key Scripture passages teach about the doctrine of inspiration? How would you define inspiration for a new Christian? How would you explain the process of inspiration to a new Christian?
Assessment	Write one-paragraph answers to the three questions and post them to Assignment #1 on the Canvas course site ***at least one hour before the class session begins***.
	In-Class Learning Space
Overview	Mini-lectures and small group discussions will help you refine your understanding of the details of the doctrine of inspiration.
Goal(s)	After you have completed the assigned learning tasks, you will have • Explained the concept of verbal plenary inspiration. • Categorized the properties of Scripture that result from inspiration. • Distinguished inspiration from revelation and illumination.
Resource(s)	Fill-in-the-blank handouts: • Theories of Inspiration • Properties Resulting from Inspiration • Revelation, Inspiration, and Illumination

Opening Stage Task	Learning Task #1: Using Poll Everywhere, take a brief "Inspiration IQ Quiz" that covers different theories of inspiration and properties that result from inspiration and discuss the results.
Middle Stage Tasks	Learning Task #2: Take notes on a mini-lecture over different theories of inspiration. Learning Task #3: Pair-Square-Share - In pairs, discuss the implications of the doctrine of verbal plenary inspiration. - With another pair, compare notes. - Share your group's findings with the rest of the class. Learning Task #4: Take notes on a mini-lecture over the properties that result from inspiration. Learning Task #5: Pair-Square-Share - In pairs, discuss the implications of each property that results from inspiration. - With another pair, compare notes. - Share your group's findings with the rest of the class. Learning Task #6: Take notes on a mini-lecture that defines revelation, inspiration, and illumination. Learning Task #7: Pair-Square-Share - In pairs, complete a table comparing revelation, inspiration, and illumination. - With another pair, compare notes. - Share your group's findings with the rest of the class.
Closing Stage Task	Learning Task #8: Using Poll Everywhere, retake the "Inspiration IQ Quiz" and discuss the results.
Assessment	Submit completed handouts for the instructor to review and return.
Post-Class Learning Space	
Overview	Assigned reading will prepare you to address apparent discrepancies in Scripture under a commitment to the verbal plenary inspiration of the Bible.
Goal(s)	After you have completed the assigned reading and tasks, you will have - Explored the implications of the doctrine of inspiration for dealing with apparent discrepancies in Scripture.
Resource(s)	Reading: McQuilkin, *Understanding and Applying the Bible*, chapter 17.

Task(s)	As you read, identify and record the presuppositions and principles that align with the doctrine of verbal plenary inspiration to use in dealing with apparent discrepancies in Scripture.
Assessment	For each set of passages below, (1) identify the apparent discrepancy(s), (2) state the principle(s) that apply, and (3) provide a possible solution to the apparent discrepancy(s). Write your answers in paragraph form with a cover page and submit them to Assignment #3 on the Canvas course site *by the day and time stated in the syllabus*. • Matthew 15:39; Mark 8:10 • Ephesians 4:10; Psalm 68:18 • Matthew 2:15; Hosea 11:1 • Matthew 20:29–34; Mark 10:46–52; Luke 18:35–43

7

Facilitating the Learning: The Design of Effective Learning-Centered Tasks

---

Chapter Preview

A learning-centered approach to instructional design emphasizes creating, implementing, and adapting learning tasks that increase engagement, improve academic outcomes, and foster meaningful, transformative learning experiences in both the classroom and online environments.

Essential questions to answer in understanding the significance of designing effective learning tasks are: (1) What best practices and principles guide the design of effective learning-centered tasks? (2) What practical guidelines support the successful implementation of the tasks? (3) What types of specific learning tasks effectively promote student engagement and learning?

The keys to designing effective learning tasks are aligning tasks with course goals, engaging learners actively, and fostering deep, meaningful learning experiences.

THE GOAL IS LEARNING, and learning tasks that engage class members actively from the outset and help them connect ideas and organize information cultivate a deeper, more lasting learning experience. Chapter 1 established the rationale for active learning and its role in promoting more meaningful educational goals. Building on that foundation, this chapter defines the learning task, offers guidelines for implementation, and presents a variety of tasks applicable in both classroom and online settings.

One of the most effective ways to help learners transfer information from working memory to long-term memory is to have them do something with what they learn. Vella defines a learning task as a structured opportunity for learners to engage actively with course content through dialogue and discovery. Instead of simply receiving information, learners respond to open-ended questions or prompts in small groups, designed to clarify and apply knowledge in meaningful ways.[1] These tasks create opportunities for exploration, clarification, and application of course content. An active approach fosters understanding that is both relevant and transformative.

The objective is "not [simply] to make learners active, but to enable them to learn what is important and meaningful."[2] The key term, *active*, means that educators must design and facilitate tasks that challenge learners to think critically and apply course material while they actively engage in problem-solving, collaboration, and reflection in ways that connect learning to real-life contexts. They need to be able to synthesize, because "the sooner the students are given opportunities to make syntheses on their own, the sooner they will feel that the world of school has something to contribute to them and to the life they will live in the wider society."[3] In other words, when learners construct meaning for themselves, it fosters personal engagement and the learning becomes more relevant.

Four Types of Learning Tasks

To foster learners' engagement and deep learning, well-structured learning tasks are essential. Vella's four types of tasks offer a natural scaffolding for introducing new content and guiding learners through the learning process:[4]

1. Inductive task
2. Input task
3. Implementation task
4. Integration task

An *inductive task* connects learners' prior knowledge and experiences to new content, guiding them from the familiar to the unfamiliar. It is ideal

---

1. Vella, *Taking Learning to Task*, 8.
2. Vella, *On Teaching and Learning*, 46.
3. Bloom et al., *Evaluation to Improve Learning*, 266.
4. Vella, *On Teaching and Learning*, 62–65.

for sparking curiosity and creating an emotional connection—two elements that help sustain attention and promote deeper learning. These types of tasks help class members see the relevance and meaning of the material and answer the question, "Why is this material important to the learner?" One effective strategy for inductive learning is to use a case scenario that prompts learners to recall what they already know and identify how it fits within a new situation. Common verbs associated with inductive tasks include *recall, identify,* or *share.*

An *input task* introduces new content, enabling learners to begin engaging key concepts or skills. This type of task lays the foundation for deeper understanding by addressing the question, "What does the learner need to know?" For example, an educator might show a short video or assign a brief article, then facilitate a discussion to help class members begin processing and applying the new material. Verbs that align with input tasks include *describe, examine,* and *listen.*

An *implementation task* involves immediate application of content through learning-centered strategies such as case analysis or personal reflection. Learners collaborate to explore the implications of the content they are striving to master. This phase answers the question, "What will the learner do with the content?" As Zarra reiterates, "Application brings relevance and relevance produces connections."[5] The implementation phase also supports the principle of massed practice, in which class members apply the content immediately to strengthen memory and reinforce understanding. Common verbs for implementation tasks include *demonstrate, illustrate,* or *perform.*

An *integration task* moves the content beyond the classroom, encouraging learners to reflect on how the new content shapes their knowledge, skills, and behaviors in real-life situations. They focus on application and transformation by considering the question, "What difference does this information make?" Learning-centered tasks include journaling, group reflection, or community-based projects. Verbs associated with integration tasks include *challenge, apply,* and *commit.*

To promote long-term retention, educators should revisit each of the four phases each semester. When learners engage content repeatedly—following the principle of distributed practice—they deepen their knowledge and increase the likelihood that learning is both meaningful and lasting. Understanding the four types of learning tasks provides a solid foundation for designing activities that are engaging, purposeful, intentional, well-placed, and aligned with students' needs and course objectives.

---

5. Zarra, *Entitled Generation*, 52.

Emotionally Engaging Environments

To implement principles of active and meaningful learning, educators must consider how to cultivate an environment that connects learners' emotions to course content. Zull writes, "Learning takes place through action, but it is driven by emotions."[6] Emotional engagement plays a vital role in sustaining attention, increasing intrinsic motivation, and supporting long-term memory. When learners feel emotionally connected to the material and to the people in the classroom, they are more likely to learn. Several strategies can create emotionally engaging environments to further support more transformative learning experiences.

Use humor to build rapport and reduce anxiety. Laughter "release[s] natural chemicals called endorphins into their blood, producing a feeling of euphoria."[7] When learners associate class with positive emotions, they are more likely to retain and recall course content. Positive emotions also create a stronger classroom community. Even a brief moment of shared laughter fosters connection, supports engagement, lowers emotional or relational barriers, and reinforces the idea that learning is both meaningful and enjoyable.

Leverage the power of storytelling. Storytelling engages areas of the brain associated with emotions, increasing motivation to listen, recall information, empathize, and connect with others.[8] Stories can evoke strong feelings such as joy, surprise, gratitude, or empathy. These emotions can deepen engagement and support memory retention and personal transformation. When learners connect the central message of a story to their experiences, they take greater ownership of the learning process, which can lead to changes in knowledge, skills, and behaviors. Educators who share stories "make learning relevant, personal, and practical. They humanize the teacher to the class."[9] Stories that engage learners' emotions can introduce a problem, clarify key concepts, demonstrate relevance, or illustrate how to apply the content. For example, in a course on spiritual formation, class members might share their testimonies of becoming Christians and how their relationship with Christ continues to mature.

Incorporate music. Choosing music that is contextually appropriate to learning goals and to different types of activities can influence mood, stimulate curiosity, and support memory retention. Studies suggest that playing

---

6. Zull, *Changing the Brain*, 54.
7. Sousa, *Rewired Brain*, 43.
8. Taylor, "Emotional Engagement," 1352–53.
9. Zarra, *Entitled Generation*, 102.

background music, without lyrics, can improve retention and enhance visuospatial skills.[10] Educators can play slower music to encourage reflection or upbeat music to energize class members before a game-based or interactive task. In certain contexts, instrumental music can also serve as cues for transitions between activities or help set the tone at the beginning of class.

Include images to deepen comprehension. Visuals capture learners' attention, and research suggests that "between 80 to 90 percent of all information that is absorbed by [the] brain is visual."[11] Because they prefer to process information more visually, integrating meaningful images is especially important for Gen Z learners. The widespread use of digital communication—especially texting—leads individuals across all generations to rely frequently on icons, emojis, and symbols to convey meaning quickly and efficiently. Studies also show that "information with rich sensory associations tends to be better remembered."[12] Presenting both visual and verbal information simultaneously—a technique known as "dual coding"—enhances the brain's ability to process and store information more effectively.[13]

Include art projects. Art-based assignments offer another form of visual engagement. For example, class members can draw symbols, create memes, or draw pictures to represent key concepts or the main idea of a lesson. These practices engage the brain's right hemisphere, activating emotions, stimulating creativity, deepening critical thinking, increasing retention, and fostering enthusiasm for the subject matter.

Enhance engagement through technology. Educators can deepen emotional and cognitive engagement by incorporating interactive tools such as polls, surveys, or online quizzes. Smartphones give class members easy access to videos, blogs, websites, or other digital resources that support in-class tasks or assignments. In addition to using technology to create digital content, as part of a learning task it can reinforce understanding through synthesis and creativity.

Incorporate gamified tools and digital games. Gamified tools and digital games can further increase motivation, enhance engagement, and foster enjoyment in the learning process. Action games activate the brain's alert and reward systems, sharpening concentration and improving critical thinking skills. They can also serve as viable options for reviewing or assessing comprehension.[14] When they incorporate games or simulations,

---

10. Sousa, *Rewired Brain*, 44.
11. Jensen, *Brain-Based Learning*, 55.
12. Miller, *Minds Online*, 95.
13. Goodwin and Marzano, *New Classroom Instruction*, 41.
14. Dehaene, *How We Learn*, 152–53.

educators should prioritize options that encourage self-competition rather than ranking. Although competition might stimulate short-term motivation for some learners, it can discourage others who feel anxious or intimidated by the pressure of the competition. Educators can address the issue by prioritizing self-competition over peer competition. If a game has a winner, design first place as demonstrating mastery of the content. Appendix G lists several technology tools educators can use in the classroom.

Use artificial intelligence judiciously. Artificial intelligence (AI) also offers opportunities for enhancing learning when educators integrate it ethically, cautiously, and within clear educational guidelines. Tools like "ChatGPT can enhance critical thinking by facilitating quick access to diverse perspectives, aiding information analysis, and supporting argument construction."[15] For example, educators might integrate ChatGPT as a tool to evaluate AI's responses in a theological debate, suggest resources for a research topic, or create images for a PowerPoint presentation.

AI tools, however, can hallucinate by generating information that is not factually correct but sounds plausible. Educators can leverage this limitation as an opportunity to help learners sharpen their skills of verifying and discerning whether something is true or fabricated. At the same time, both critics and advocates of AI warn that overreliance on these tools can inhibit self-reflection, reduce intrinsic motivations, and hinder critical thinking skills. AI should not replace academic rigor or other learning strategies. Educators should use discernment when integrating AI into their curricular designs to ensure that class members remain active, self-directed learners rather than passive recipients of AI-generated content.

Ask emotionally reflective questions. Questions such as "Why does this idea matter to you?" or "How does this concept align with what you have experienced?" allow learners the opportunity to reflect on their values, emotions, and past experiences. For example, during a discussion on the theology of suffering, these questions can lead to deeper dialogue about how loss or grief affects them personally. Engaging the emotions first helps learners transition more naturally to cognitive or behavioral domains during class discussions.

Effective Discussion Questions

Discussion is a key component of any active learning task. Well-crafted questions can promote observation, interpretation, and application of content and can help class members reach deeper levels of critical thinking and

---

15. Melisa et al., "Critical Thinking," 1.

recall. The following eight guidelines help craft questions that foster engagement and critical thinking:

1. Align questions with goals.
2. Ask open-ended questions.
3. Be clear and concise.
4. Use a variety of question types.
5. Eliminate filler questions.
6. Divide run-on questions.
7. Avoid leading questions.
8. Avoid answering questions.

The following table expands the guidelines and offers examples:

Guideline	Description and Example
Align questions with goals.	Connect questions to course and class goals in order to maintain relevance and direction. *Poor*: What do you think about today's topic? *Better*: How does the topic of suffering fit with the overall objective of reviewing theological principles of sanctification?
Ask open-ended questions.	Ask questions that invite more than a yes or no answer. *Poor*: Is there a difference between active and passive learning? *Better*: How would you explain the difference between active and passive learning?
Be clear and concise.	Avoid complex or confusing wording. *Poor*: What is the distinct divergence between the pedagogical methods of active and passive learning, particularly in regard to cognitive processing involvement and the degree to which learner autonomy dominates the overall educational experience? *Better*: What is the difference between active and passive learning?
Use a variety of question types.	Include questions at different levels of learning and in different domains of learning. *Poor*: What are the four elements of a learning task? *Better*: How would you design a fifteen-minute learning task that incorporates the four elements of Vella's model?

Eliminate filler questions.	Avoid vague prompts that do not foster engagement. *Poor*: Any questions? *Better*: If you had to describe a learning task to a friend, what part would be the hardest to explain?
Divide run-on questions.	Break complex, multi-part questions into manageable parts. *Poor*: How do learning tasks help students apply this idea to real life, do you think they are better than lectures, and how would you use them in class? *Better*: How do learning tasks encourage real-life application? What are some strengths or limitations of using learning tasks rather than lectures? How would you incorporate learning tasks in class?
Avoid leading questions.	Avoid guiding students toward a particular answer. *Poor*: Don't you think learning tasks are more effective than lectures? *Better*: What are the strengths and limitations of using learning tasks compared to lectures?
Avoid answering questions.	Do not answer questions. Wait at least five seconds to give class members time to process. Rephrase the question if necessary. *Poor*: The answer is that . . . *Better*: Let me ask the question in a different way . . .

Small Group Learning

Another valuable component of a learning-centered task is small group work. While well-crafted questions stimulate meaningful class-wide dialogue, small groups offer a structured space for deeper exploration and peer interaction. In small groups, class members have the opportunity to engage various viewpoints, practice communication and collaboration, and cultivate a sense of community. Lawson observes, "Cooperative learning produces higher achievement, more positive relationships among students, and healthier psychological adjustment than do competitive or individualistic experiences."[16] Instead of passively receiving information, learners actively dialogue with others to find solutions, test ideas, and debate multiple perspectives. The process develops both cognitive and interpersonal skills. As Taylor and Marienau emphasize, learners must verbalize the content in order to recognize that learning has occurred and to understand how it has changed their beliefs and behaviors.[17]

16. Lawson, *Professor's Puzzle*, 173.
17. Taylor and Marienau, *Facilitating Learning*, 84.

Small group work also increases learners' sense of autonomy and ownership. When they collaborate on meaningful tasks, they take greater responsibility for shared conclusions. To support these outcomes, educators should arrange tables or chairs in a circle or half-circle so that students can easily hear, see, and collaborate with one another. Shifting the focal point of the classroom also reinforces the educator's role as a facilitator rather than a lecturer. Periodically varying the room setup can help sustain curiosity and engagement.

Effective learning begins with knowing the learners—understanding their needs, motivations, and how they engage meaningfully with course content. Educators should consider how small groups, or any learning-centered strategy, support three core drivers of motivation in order to evaluate the effectiveness of the task. Pink notes that three principles serve as a foundation for designing transformative learning experiences that prepare learners to apply knowledge, skills, and behaviors to real-life settings:[18]

1. Autonomy: Does the task allow learners to make meaningful choices about how or when to complete the work?
2. Mastery: Does the task promote depth of understanding rather than rote memorization?
3. Purpose: Is the task clearly connected to a broader goal, whether personal, academic, or spiritual?

To maximize the benefits of small group work, educators should include learners with diverse backgrounds, nationalities, generations, cultures, and social contexts in the groups. Diversity in groups can teach important lessons about collaboration and cooperation while reinforcing the importance of working toward a shared goal. A practical strategy for promoting both structure and autonomy is assigning roles within the group. This strategy ensures that each member contributes, distributes responsibility, and sets clear expectations for group interaction. The roles should align with the task's goals and be appropriate to the group size. Rotating roles from task to task allows group members to develop a range of competencies, including communication, collaboration, and leadership. The following table provides examples of different group roles and their purposes:

---

18. Pink, *Drive*, 175.

Facilitating the Learning: The Design of Effective Learning-Centered Tasks   137

Small Group Roles	
Analyst	Brings alternatives, perspectives, tests assumptions, and introduces new approaches.
Director	Manages time, oversees deadlines, and maintains steady progress.
Liaison	Obtains resources and relays questions or updates to the instructor or to other groups during the task.
Mediator	Encourages collaboration, resolves tensions, and fosters consensus.
Moderator	Guides discussion, promotes participation, and keeps the group on track.
Notetaker	Records notes that capture key points, decisions, and next steps.
Organizer	Clarifies objectives, defines priorities, and structures workflow.
Presenter	Communicates conclusions and insights to the instructor and/or the class.
Researcher	Locates relevant resources, examples, or additional information.
Reviewer	Confirms accuracy, verifies understanding, and validates accuracy of information.

    Learners are most engaged when they understand what they are learning, why it matters, and how they will participate in the process. According to Goodwin and Marzano, "When students know what they will learn . . . why they [are] learning it . . . and how they will engage in learning and monitoring their progress . . . it provides a clear pathway and motivation for learning."[19]

    Before implementing specific learning tasks, educators also need to consider where to place each activity within the overall course structure. Sustaining learners' attention throughout a class session can be challenging. Strategic timing of learning tasks is crucial for maximizing engagement and comprehension. Transitions between passive and active learning modalities can help re-engage class members. Conversely, beginning with an active task, such as demonstrations and polls, can boost attention and focus during a subsequent lecture segment.

    Attention naturally wanes over time. The brain follows a rest-activity cycle that typically requires a break around the ninety-minute mark. In

---

19. Goodwin and Marzano, *New Classroom Instruction*, 35.

longer class periods, cognitive fatigue becomes a probability and incorporating brief pauses for stretching or rest helps class members regain focus and sustain engagement. To sustain attention and prevent instructional monotony, educators should incorporate a variety of approaches. Varying the balance between passive and active strategies sustains a sense of curiosity without overwhelming class members through constant change. The following example is a schedule for a blocked class with time allocations and active learning strategies that include Vella's four parts of a learning task:

Schedule for a Three-Hour Blocked Class Session	
1:30–1:40	Inductive Task: Writing prompt to connect prior knowledge
1:40–1:50	Debrief
1:50–2:10	Lecture: Preview new content
2:10–2:25	Input Task: Video and small group comprehension questions
2:25–2:35	Debrief
2:35–2:50	Break
2:50–3:05	Implementation Task: Case study
3:05–3:25	Debrief: Group reports
3:25–3:45	Lecture: Clarify key concepts
3:45–3:55	Integration Task: Think-Pair-Share on how content applies to life
3:55–4:05	Assessment of Learning: Exit ticket
4:05–4:15	Wrap-Up: Summary of key points and assignment questions

This approach reflects what Newton describes as "the integration of solid content [with] both analytical and experiential learning. Deeper learning happens when developmentally appropriate content is absorbed through interactive, active, and experiential approaches."[20] The sample schedule demonstrates the balance of blending content delivery with activities that require learners to analyze, discuss, and apply what they are learning. Learning tasks reveal whether class members understand the material and can adapt it to fit their context. As Wiggins observes, "Good design will establish the idea that there will be a clear need for the learner to make sense of what the teacher teaches."[21]

20. Newton, *Heart-Deep Teaching*, 166.
21. Wiggins and McTighe, *Understanding by Design*, 103.

Before the Task

To achieve a higher level of engagement and relevancy during a task, educators must begin by understanding their learners, articulating measurable learning goals, and developing content that aligns with both learners' needs and course goals. Learning tasks represent the culminating step in designing a learning-centered instructional approach. Developing meaningful tasks is challenging. Educators must consider multiple factors to ensure the activity facilitates deep, transformative experiences. Vella suggests using seven questions to structure a lesson: Who? Why? When? Where? What? What for? and How?[22] With some rewording and reordering these seven questions form the basis for a Task Design Guide:

1. What are the needs, interests, and abilities of the learners?
2. What specific concepts, skills, or knowledge should the learners understand or apply?
3. Why is the content important for the learners?
4. Does the task align with the course goals?
5. What is the time limit for the task?
6. What is the learning environment?
7. What materials does the task require?

The following table presents each question, provides a sample response, and explains the significance of the question for the lesson planning:

Task Design Guide		
Question	Sample Response	Significance
What are the needs, interests, and abilities of the learners?	Class members are between the ages of twenty-four and forty-five; ten are from US, four are from China, one is from Africa; they have varying levels of prior knowledge.	Knowing the learners allows the educator to tailor the task to ensure engagement and provide an appropriate level of challenge.

---

22. Vella, *On Teaching and Learning*, 31.

What specific concepts, skills, or knowledge should the students understand or apply?	The objective is to write an observation, interpretation, and application questions that foster meaningful thinking and dialogue in a Bible lesson.	This ensures the task addresses key concepts and skills to reinforce the course objectives.
Why is the content important for the learners?	After analyzing a passage of Scripture, class members should be able to create observation, interpretation, and application questions for a Bible lesson, which is crucial for future leadership in church or ministry contexts.	Demonstrating relevancy increases student motivation and helps them see the task's value for their future ministry.
Does the task align with course goals?	The task directly contributes to the course outcome of incorporating interactive, inductive, question-based strategies to promote active engagement.	Aligning the task with course outcomes ensures its purpose and facilitates assessment of students' progress toward the learning goals.
What is the time limit for the task?	Allot two thirty-minute time slots for the task.	The time period ensures the task is manageable and allows time for meaningful debriefing.
What is the learning environment?	The classroom includes movable desks, a projector, and a whiteboard.	An assessment of the environment ensures that the resources and space support effective learning.
What materials does the task require?	The materials include Bibles, handouts, paper, and pencils.	Ensuring materials are available eliminates confusion and barriers to participation.

Once the educator selects an appropriate task for class members, the next step is to finalize the timing and structure. Finalizing an effective learning task includes five key elements.

First, *set the time*. Determine the exact amount of time required for class members to complete the task. Set a clear ending time—for example, "Complete the task by 10:15 a.m." Estimating task duration accurately is essential; too much time can cause the energy level of the class to drop, while too little time can lead to frustration.

Second, *adjust the complexity*. Adjust the task's complexity according to the learners' stage of learning. Early tasks may involve foundational comprehension, while later tasks should involve higher-level analysis, synthesis, and application. See appendix H for different levels of complexity.

Third, *include repetition*. Consider how many times class members should engage the content to reinforce understanding. Repetition through varied formats strengthens retention. In most cases, requiring learners to demonstrate or apply a new skill at least three times significantly increases the likelihood of mastery.

Fourth, *form small groups*. Design groups to optimize participation by all members. Typically, groups of three to five class members work well for promoting individual accountability and meaningful collaboration.

Fifth, *give clear instructions*. Provide clear, detailed directions. Directions should briefly explain the task and its relevance to learners, outline how to form groups, and define specific roles such as reporter or presenter.

When the task involves multiple steps or complex content, prepare a handout outlining all expectations. Before the class members begin the task, always ask, "Does everyone understand what to do?" This simple yet effective question check helps prevent confusion about group roles, task steps, or time limits. By addressing these five factors—duration, complexity, repetition, group structure, and instructions—educators can implement learning-centered tasks that are well-structured, engaging, and conducive to deep learning.

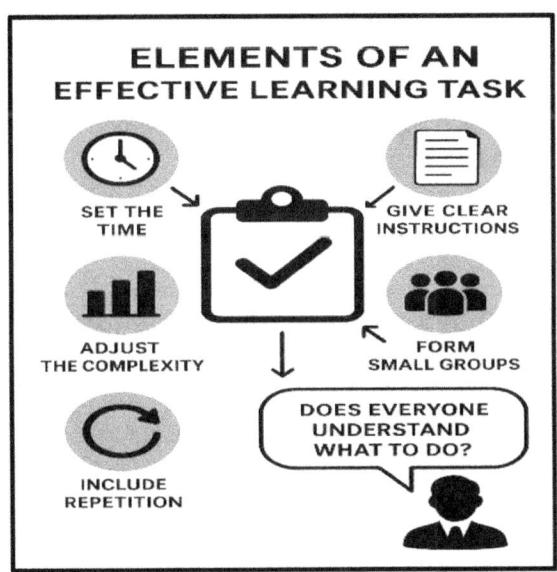

During the Task

Once it is clear that class members understand the instructions, the task can begin. This moment marks the point at which learners start to "actively 'uncover' what lies below the surface of the facts . . . to ponder their meaning."[23] During the task, the educator serves as a facilitator and circulates throughout the room to answer questions, clarify instructions, redirect groups that stray off-track, and encourage deeper engagement with the content. It is important to observe nonverbal cues for signs of confusion or disengagement, monitor participation, and intervene if a group becomes stuck or uncertain about how to proceed. Observing participation levels and intervening at appropriate times helps maintain momentum and keeps learners on track. Periodic time reminders (e.g., "one minute remaining," "thirty seconds left") helps class members pace their time and conclude the task effectively. Most of the dialogue during the task, however, should take place between the learners, because peer-to-peer interaction is key to active learning.

After the Task

Once learners complete the task, it is essential to set aside time to debrief. Learning does not occur through experience alone but through the process of reflecting on that experience and drawing meaning from it.[24] Debriefing offers learners an opportunity to reflect on their learning, clarify confusion, and connect the task to real-life contexts and course objectives. A time of reflection aids the transfer of knowledge into long-term memory and prepares class members to apply the concepts in new situations. A thorough debrief typically includes several essential components:

Elements of a Thorough Debrief	
Review the purpose of the task.	Reiterate why they completed the task and how it connects to the course objectives or real-life applications.
Ask open-ended questions.	Encourage deeper thinking by asking evaluative and application-based questions that prompt observation, interpretation, and application.

---

23. Wiggins and McTighe, *Understanding by Design*, 103.
24. Dewey, *Experience and Education*, 25.

Give positive feedback.	Acknowledge learners' contributions to affirm effort, build confidence, and reinforce key insights.
Process misunderstandings.	Allow time to explore areas of confusion, answer questions, and provide instructional points or examples to solidify understanding.
Summarize the task.	Recap the key ideas, concepts, and applications; connect observations, interpretations, and applications to the broader course themes and future learning opportunities.

Learning-Centered Strategies

There are a range of principles and learning tasks that educators can use to promote engagement, foster motivation, and support learners in applying new content in ways that transform their knowledge, skills, and behavior. The following list organizes strategies in alphabetical order for quick reference and includes a brief explanation of each task. Although it is not exhaustive, the list serves as a starting point for creating a more engaging learning-centered classroom environment. Many strategies can support multiple purposes, such as developing critical thinking, increasing motivation, improving communication skills, or building community, depending on how the instructor frames and facilitates the task. Appendix F includes additional options and descriptions.

When choosing learning-centered tasks, educators should remember that "variety and novelty are key to re-engaging students' brains,"[25] particularly as attention begins to diminish. In addition to selecting the right strategy, educators can encourage autonomy by incorporating meaningful choices within the task itself. Overall, the strategies below offer practical, adaptable options for designing learning-centered tasks that incorporate variety, sustain attention, boost autonomy, and motivate learners toward deeper, more lasting learning.

Brainstorming exercises present learners with challenges and ask them to generate multiple practical solutions. Brainstorming encourages divergent thinking in which class members must generate multiple responses rather than searching for a single correct answer. Learners explore different perspectives, apply prior knowledge, and practice problem-solving, which

---

25. Goodwin and Marzano, *New Classroom Instruction*, 81.

supports the development of important critical thinking and metacognitive awareness.

Case studies are structured scenarios based on real-life situations that illustrate the application of course content in context. They help "students see the why, where, when, and how content is important."[26] Educators can use case studies to encourage learners to reflect, analyze, and synthesize. The objective is not to reach a single correct answer, but to explore a range of ideas and perspectives that lead to transformed knowledge, skills, or behaviors. Case studies support the development of critical thinking skills and might uncover new insights, challenge misconceptions, or prompt a call to action.

Gallery walks encourage movement, collaboration, and reflection as class members respond to prompts on posted charts or boards and reflect on others' responses. Before class, the educator writes questions or statements on flip chart paper posted on walls or whiteboards. Learners walk around the room and post their answers or comments on the papers. After an allotted amount of time, they can browse the room and look at the postings of their classmates.

Highs and lows sharing encourages reflection, clarifies misunderstandings, and identifies learning challenges. After covering key concepts, class members share a "high"—something that was interesting, meaningful, or thought-provoking—and a "low"—something that was confusing, difficult, or boring. In large classes, learners can share their highs and lows in groups of three or four, while the educator rotates among the groups.

Icebreakers help establish a welcoming classroom environment and help class members learn their peers' names and discover shared interests. Introductions and icebreakers can reduce anxiety, foster a sense of belonging, and lay the foundation for community spirit. For an introductory icebreaker, the educator can ask class members to share where they are from and one interest or hobby they enjoy doing outside of class. The activity encourages connection and builds student rapport with one another. For a creative icebreaker, each class member can draw a meme, share a GIF, or select a movie clip that represents his or her personality. Classmates guess whom they think each item represents. The activity fosters familiarity and emotional engagement, which enhances attention, memory, and participation.

Interviews cultivate listening and communication skills as well as encouraging inquiry, empathy, and personal engagement with the course content. When class members interview individuals from different generations or cultural backgrounds to broaden their perspective, the task can expand

---

26. Boettcher and Conrad, *Online Teaching Survival Guide*, 291.

appreciation of different generational, cultural, or social viewpoints and experiences.

Jigsaws encourage communication, responsibility, and collaborative learning. A jigsaw is a cooperative learning-centered strategy designed to develop a more comprehensive understanding of a topic. Each member of a group researches a portion of the larger topic. After doing their own research, they meet with their peers in one of the other groups who have studied the same portion of the topic and compare notes. Once they believe that they understand the topic, they go back to their group and present the information.

Journals provide opportunities for quiet reflection through written responses to a question prompt. Journaling promotes metacognition and critical thinking by allowing learners the opportunity to evaluate their learning and make personal connections to the material.

Motivation exchanges can help educators better understand class members' motivations so that they can tailor examples, applications, or discussions accordingly. At the beginning of the course, each learner responds in writing to a series of reflective questions such as, What is the purpose of this course? What do you hope to accomplish or master in this course? How is the course relevant to the world today? They then share their responses with a partner and submit them to the instructor.

One-minute papers help educators assess comprehension and identify areas that need clarification or more exploration. At the end of a class session, learners have one minute to respond briefly to content-focused or application-focused questions about what they learned from the class.

Pair-square-share tasks reinforce reflective thinking, collaborative learning, critical thinking, and confidence in sharing ideas. Students begin by reflecting on a question or prompt, then discuss their ideas with a partner (pair). Each pair then joins another pair to form a group of four (square) and discusses their responses. Finally, groups share key insights with the whole class (share).

Peer and self-evaluations provide valuable feedback, promote awareness of accountability, and create an opportunity to discuss topics such as teamwork and group dynamics, which are essential skills to a healthy community atmosphere. During or after group projects, class members assess their own contributions and the contributions of the group. Providing rubrics to complete or questions to answer can help learners in appraising collaboration, communication, and responsibility.

Polls can increase engagement and provide immediate information as a way to address any confusion or misunderstandings. Using classroom response tools or polling apps to collect feedback can help assess prior knowledge, check mid-lesson for understanding, enhance participation, or reinforce key concepts.

Presentations encourage ownership, build confidence, facilitate synthesis of learning, and challenge learners to think critically about how to present material for engagement and understanding. One of the most effective ways to demonstrate individual mastery of a subject is to teach it to someone else. One option it to assign topics related to the course content to research and present to the class. To encourage autonomy, another option is to allow class members to select topics that align with their personal interests or have relevance to their experiences.

Projects are an effective way to build community and collaboration over an extended period of time. They are also effective in building teamwork, time management, and problem-solving skills. Providing clear instructions that outline the scope and sequence of the project, along with formatting and rubrics, is essential. Breaking the project into smaller, scaffolded components provides guidance and reduces cognitive overload. Instructions that include checklists, sample projects, or short video guidelines help clarify expectations and reduce frustration and anxiety.

Role plays can promote deeper engagement with social, cultural, or ethical issues related to the course content. For example, in a church history or theology course, class members could take on the roles of John Calvin and Martin Luther, who debate topics on salvation or church authority. Learners engage in a scenario or discussion with or without prescribed lines for various purposes, such as experiencing other perspectives, practicing a new skill, reinforcing comprehension, and encouraging students to engage in complex or unfamiliar viewpoints.

Tea parties can review key concepts and facilitate peer interaction. Each learner receives a color-coded index card with a question related to the lesson. Class members circulate around the room asking and answering questions of peers who hold different colored cards. They record their classmates' responses before rotating to another learner.

Think-pair-share tasks promote participation, reinforce understanding, and encourage both reflective and collaborative thinking. First, learners take time to reflect individually on a question (think). They then pair with a classmate to discuss their responses (pair). Finally, pairs have opportunities to share their discoveries with the rest of the class (share).

Writing prompts engage various levels of learning to help clarify concepts, encourage analysis, and connect to prior knowledge. After listening to a lecture or reading, learners write a brief summary or response to a specific prompt. Then, they compare their summaries with a classmate. The physical act of moving the pen across the paper also transfers the information more easily into long-term memories.

Conclusion

Yount stresses that effective teaching incorporates both art and science. The educator becomes an artist who "weave[s] together competing elements—content and communication, justice and grace, control and nurture, challenge and support—in order to help learners grow."[27] The educator also functions as a scientist who "investigates the most effective ways to create positive learning environments, address learner differences, and engage learners' head, heart, and hand."[28]

Educators must learn to weave together course content with learning tasks that best support learners. When these two elements—thoughtful content and purposeful learning-centered strategies—work together, education becomes transformational. Learners gain knowledge, behaviors, and skills that not only change their academic development but also foster spiritual and emotional growth.

Food for Thought
How can you determine which learning-centered strategies are most appropriate for a given lesson or group of learners?
How can you adapt learning tasks to learners' needs, time constraints, or class size?
What new learning tasks can you incorporate into one of your courses in order to promote engagement while also meeting course goals?

---

27. Yount, *Created to Learn*, 1.
28. Yount, *Created to Learn*, 1.

8

Delivering the Learning: The Opportunities of Online Learning

Chapter Preview
The online modality creates unique challenges and opportunities for educators who focus on learning.
A blended format for an online course balances the tension of a learner's need for flexibility, connection, and engagement.
A learning-centered approach to delivering higher education explores using existing and emerging technologies as powerful tools for both educators and learners to enhance accessibility, engagement, and personalized learning experiences.

THE GOAL IS LEARNING, and focusing on learning means always adapting to learners' needs. The fundamental needs of the learner might not vary significantly from generation to generation, but learners' expectations shift. Accessibility remains a core need for the learner. Over the last fifteen years, nontraditional students have increased to the point of constituting the majority of college students in the United States.[1] A nontraditional college student is older than twenty-four and is studying part time.[2] The sheer volume of nontraditional learners underscores the need for flexible learning

---

1. Leggins, "'New' Nontraditional Students," 35.
2. Remenick, "Nontraditional Students," 113.

formats and modalities. Adapting to learners' needs means meeting them where they are, whether relationally or even physically.

The educator who focuses on learners' needs also uses every available tool to serve the learning process, and those tools constantly change. Although chalkboards or calculators might have been the height of innovation in their time, learning-focused educators seek out new tools and technologies. They do not abandon older tools for every new innovation, but they remain open to new learning modalities and technologies.

Both of these principles of learning-centered teaching—adapting to needs and utilizing available tools—make it natural that the learning-focused educator embraces online instruction. Online learning gives access to learners who would otherwise not have the opportunity to pursue higher education. Online learning also meets learners through a medium that has become native to them. The learning-focused educator seeks to leverage the online modality to enhance learning.

The Background of Online Learning

The National Center for Education Statistics reports that in the past twenty years, colleges and universities have increasingly turned to online learning as a means to meet the challenge of an increasingly nontraditional student population. For just undergraduate studies in the United States, online enrollment, where the student's entire degree program is completed online, has jumped from 4.9 million in 2003 to 23.9 million in 2019.[3]

In the earliest days of distance instruction, higher education institutions modeled instruction on former distance education models where the student would mail in work and watch recorded materials. Accelerated by the COVID pandemic, institutions implemented online instruction as a necessity. With students unable to come to campus, colleges and universities shifted to online platforms as a way to maintain access to instruction without physical presence. Now, the number of online learners rivals that of residential learners. Even learners who are studying residentially are likely to take online courses as a way to simplify their schedules or accelerate their studies.

Fundamental to online learning is an educational framework that emphasizes a constructivist and problem-based learning philosophy. In an online course, learners actively generate ideas and contribute to the learning environment. Self-direction and active learning become imperative for an

---

3. Digest of Education Statistics, "Table 311.22"

effective online course. Educators' strategies and approaches shift to those of motivator and guide through the online learning experience.

The Opportunities of Online Learning

For colleges and universities, online learning creates entirely new opportunities to serve students. Higher education has leveraged the online modality to meet the students' need for increased accessibility. Online learning addresses the issue of access to physical learning environments by allowing learners to study from miles, time zones, or even countries away. Colleges and universities are no longer limited to serving learners who have the means and flexibility to live within physical proximity of the educational institution. Instead, online learning brings learning to learners.

Access refers not only to physical access, but also to flexibility and pacing. Online instruction often allows learners to engage material and their classmates at their own pace and on their own schedule. Learners of nontraditional age or life circumstance can still access higher education. This accessibility opens higher education to learners with additional responsibilities than the typical, traditional-aged student might have. Whether a learner is trying to balance studying with working full time or parenting, online learning opens up new possibilities for them.

Online instruction also increases access through more affordable pricing. Colleges and universities often price online courses and programs at a lower rate than residential equivalents. Institutions are able to keep prices down for online learners because of the limited overhead required for the programs. Lower tuition costs, along with not relocating to a campus location or limiting employment, mean greater access for the online learner.

Educators also gain new opportunities with the online modality. Previously limited to teaching only learners who could physically come to their classrooms, educators were only able to teach learners with physical access to a campus. Educators now educate across the globe and can teach from anywhere in the world. This flexibility creates entirely new opportunities for learning. Learners and educators bring cultural and practical experiences to the virtual classroom regardless of proximity to a local campus.

The Challenges of Online Learning

Colleges and universities achieve their primary objective to increase access through online instruction. Learners gain access to learning they would otherwise never achieve. Educators embrace the new opportunity of teaching in a global classroom. The expanding world of online instruction opens all of these opportunities, but an online modality also includes several inherent challenges to learning. Educators face challenges unique to the online modality, requiring adaptability and flexibility to achieve learning outcomes while utilizing nontraditional methods. Learners also face challenges in an online modality.

Although online instruction overcomes accessibility issues on many fronts, technology gaps might still exist. Technology has become ubiquitous in today's society, but learners still face the challenge of access to appropriate technology for online instruction. Online learning requires more than a smartphone, and a significant number of learners will struggle to have ongoing access to a computer with more robust word processing abilities. Even those learners who are academically ready for college-level work might find the technology necessary for online learning challenging.

Learners often bring unrealistic expectations to online learning. Since other online environments, from social media to e-commerce, are built for immediate results, learners make similar demands of online learning. They expect grading to be instantaneous, email replies to come within minutes, and courses to suit their preferences. They might not necessarily explicitly name these expectations, but the modern environment creates them. Many educators face these same unrealistic expectations in residential campus environments, but the online environment exaggerates them. Furthermore, learning platforms that mirror other online platforms reinforce expectations of immediacy.

Perhaps the most compelling and concerning challenge for online learning is the potential lack of personal connection that learners experience in many online courses and programs. Residential courses, even large sections held in college auditoriums, allow for face-to-face interactions and connections. Many online courses and programs depend on class members working almost entirely autonomously. Self-directed learning is a cornerstone of the online format, but low retention and graduation rates for online learners underscore the unique challenges that they face.

The Formats for Online Learning

Not all online learning experiences are the same. Institutions and educators aim to mitigate some of the challenges inherent to online learning by adopting different approaches to the format of online instruction. Institutions use three different approaches:

1. Fully asynchronous format
2. Fully synchronous format
3. Blended format

In order to maximize student flexibility and student access, many colleges and universities adopt a *fully asynchronous format* for their online courses and programs. Assignments have specific deadlines within a week, but class members work on the assignments at any time within the week. Typically, learners participate in discussion boards that enable them to interact with one another through threaded posts on the learning management system (LMS). Discussion boards make it possible to simulate classroom interactions without scheduling live sessions, which can be challenging or impossible for adult learners studying across various time zones. This approach prioritizes the needs of the adult learner for flexibility and access.

On the opposite end of the spectrum, some colleges and universities adopt *a fully synchronous format* for their online instruction. In this approach, class members participate in required live virtual sessions. The virtual sessions directly simulate an in-person class experience. For some courses, this approach might mean that online learners join an in-person class virtually. Through synchronous instruction, institutions and educators aim to combat several of the challenges of online instruction by offering a real-time connection. For some learners, the synchronous format meets their needs, while for others, the challenge of scheduling and access makes this format impossible.

A *blended format* seeks to balance the advantages and disadvantages of asynchronous and synchronous online instruction. In a blended format, learners have flexibility in when they work on assignments, but they also have the opportunity for greater connection through virtual sessions together. Essentially, a blended format offers live, albeit virtual, interactions with the flexibility of personalized scheduling or alternative assignments when scheduling is a barrier.

Although the blended format includes synchronous elements, the format acknowledges the need for flexibility. To achieve flexibility, the majority of the course uses an asynchronous format. Learners are able to work independently, balancing employment and family obligations. What is available in synchronous format is available virtually through virtual meeting technologies (e.g., Zoom, Teams) or directly through the university LMS. These virtual sessions simulate in-class meetings through live discussion, aiming to create connection and engagement. Often, to meet class members' needs for flexibility, meetings are less frequent than residential class meetings.

Whatever structure blended formats might use, the aim is to balance the learner's need for flexibility and access with the benefits provided by real-time interaction.

Online Course Formats		
Fully Asynchronous	Fully Synchronous	Hybrid
<ul><li>No times to meet live</li><li>Interaction through threaded posts</li><li>Priority to flexibility and access</li></ul>	<ul><li>Fixed times to meet live</li><li>Interaction through real-time sessions</li><li>Priority to connection and engagement</li></ul>	<ul><li>Flexible times to meet live</li><li>Interaction through real-time sessions</li><li>Priority to balance of flexibility and connection</li></ul>

Regardless of the format, the educator's goal remains the same—to facilitate learning. Many of the tools and skills the educator might utilize in a physical classroom are not available in a virtual environment. Without these traditional tools, online educators face a unique challenge in creating and leading an online course. They must contextualize teaching and learning strategies to the online modality. Effective online educators embrace creativity and adaptability to achieve learning outcomes using new tools and strategies to meet the new challenge and opportunity of online learning.

Designing Online Learning with the End in Mind

Designing a learning-centered course begins and ends with the learning goals. The online course is no different. The online educator designs each element, assignment, and task in order to achieve the learning goals for the course. The following is an example of course goals for a Strategic Planning course at the graduate level. Previous chapters have set out the benefits of articulating goals in terms of what learners will have accomplished by the end of the course.

> Sample Goals for a Strategic Planning Course
>
> ***By the end of this course, you will have***
>
> **Described** the importance of developing a clear strategic vision within an organization. (Remember/Understand)
>
> **Assessed** the leader's role in cultivating culture, aligning values, and ensuring strategy implementation. (Evaluate)
>
> **Evaluated** the connections among ethics, social responsibility, and long-term organizational sustainability. (Evaluate)
>
> **Analyzed** organizations' internal and external environments to inform strategic objectives. (Analyze)
>
> **Formulated** effective organizational strategies using appropriate planning techniques and frameworks. (Apply/Create)
>
> **Designed** an implementation plan for executing organizational strategies effectively. (Create)

Leveraging Tools to Achieve the Goals of Online Learning

The preceding goals are not unique to the online modality. The educator begins with the end in mind and—if teaching in an online modality—utilizes certain tools to facilitate the learning. The residential educator utilizes these same tools, but the online educator finds unique ways to leverage each of them. Careful planning for achieving learning in an online format typically involves four major tools:

1. Videos
2. Readings
3. Discussions
4. Assignments

Use videos to set the agenda for learning. In the earliest days of distance learning, recordings (eventually videos) consisted of full lectures by the faculty member. Learners would listen to or watch hours of content as a substitute for in-class learning. In today's online environment, the use and purpose of video content have evolved to meet the needs of the learner. Rather than serving as the primary source for instruction, videos now serve to introduce topics, pique interest, and point to the learning goal. This reimagining of the use of video in an online course means that the online educator leverages the tool of video in new ways to achieve this purpose.

If videos set the agenda for learning, then the length of the videos will be vastly different from the hours-long videos of early distance learning. Videos will be much shorter, lasting only three to five minutes. The educator aims to introduce a topic or learning goal concisely while maintaining interest and pointing class members to the learning that will take place in a given week or module.

With videos shortened to easily digestible lengths, the frequency of using them can vary significantly. An educator might choose to incorporate videos into weekly announcements or as a short introduction to each module. In either approach, the goal is to create cadence and flow to the course by utilizing short, engaging videos as a means of promoting interest and motivation. Because of the purpose and length of the video, the educator will focus on introducing main ideas rather than going into great detail.

Use readings to introduce new concepts and skills. In residential courses, readings can vary in their centrality to the course. Residential educators often introduce new concepts and material through face-to-face instruction, with reading reinforcing that learning. In an online course, reading becomes the essential means for introducing and exploring concepts and skills to learners. The learners' self-direction is critical to a meaningful online learning experience. This self-direction is especially demonstrated in their interactions with reading material, both in initial exposure as well as in reflecting and applying reading.

The first learning goal of the Strategic Planning course above serves as a helpful example of structuring reading around encountering key concepts. That goal is "By the end of this course, you will have described the importance of developing a clear strategic vision within an organization." The assigned reading should introduce strategic vision as a concept and explain how it serves as a driving force for an organization. The reading might define and describe the concept of strategic vision, provide examples, and compare and contrast companies' strategic vision. It might even provide an analysis of a company's vision statement, evaluating its effectiveness and execution. Once exposed to this level of introduction to the concept of vision statements through readings, learners are ready to delve deeply into the topic through discussions and assignments.

Of course, the complexity of the subject matter affects the amount of time needed to complete the reading. The following table serves as a helpful guide in balancing the amount of reading learners can reasonably complete within an hour:

Sample Reading Parameters		
Highly complex	Many new concepts	10 pages per hour
Moderately complex	Some new concepts	12 pages per hour
Popular/Scripture	No new concepts	15 pages per hour

Although reading is a central component of online courses, the total number of hours allotted to reading should not exceed half of the course workload. The goal is to encourage learning autonomy through reading, establishing a foundation of understanding of the course concepts and materials. Other learning tasks within the course are critical for exploring and expanding this learning. The volume of reading will vary with the type of course and the goals of the course.

Use dialogue and discussions to create energy and momentum. When online educators use them effectively, dialogue and discussions push learners toward deeper levels of learning, creating an opportunity to apply, analyze, and evaluate. In an online format, the learner encounters new material through introductory videos and readings. Educators tailor discussions to deepen understanding of new concepts through further exploration of the topic. Discussions serve as a low-stakes environment for reinforcing new learning as well as evaluating or contextualizing the material.

The platform and method for conducting discussions are critical to the effectiveness of the learning. Online course formats vary from asynchronous to synchronous to hybrid. The format for discussions typically determines the course type. For asynchronous courses, the LMS most likely includes a discussion board feature that allows for threaded replies. These asynchronous discussions can use written posts and responses, posted audios, or posted videos. The key to this format is that class members can post their initial thoughts and replies on their own schedule as long as they do so prior to the assigned deadline. The instructor might choose this format to maximize flexibility for learners while still achieving the learning goals. For synchronous or blended formats, platforms like Zoom and Teams serve as a virtual meeting space for live interactions. Educators can simulate the live interactions learners would experience in a physical classroom. It is possible to leverage either of these formats for discussions effectively to achieve course outcomes.

Driving to accomplish learning goals, regardless of the format of the discussion, remains the primary objective. The second goal of the Strategic Planning course provides an example of utilizing discussion to expand learning. The goal is "By the end of this course, you will have assessed the leader's role in cultivating culture, aligning values, and ensuring strategy implementation." The educator knows that a video has introduced the topic and has provided a road map for the learning that will take place in the unit. The educator has also planned for the reading to introduce concepts of culture, values, and strategy implementation. The reading might even have provided examples of assessing a leader's role in different organizations.

The next step is to leverage discussion to ensure that class members have comprehended the reading and to help them move toward higher levels of learning. The discussion prompt might include an example or case study not previously encountered in the reading and might ask class members to assess how the leader influenced culture, values, and strategy implementation. The educator could also ask learners to draw from their own experiences to illustrate the role of a leader in shaping culture. Using discussion could encourage learners to reflect on their own experiences, engage in agreeable disagreement with classmates, and utilize the reading to support conclusions.

Discussion conducted in this way becomes a key element for learners to reflect on new concepts, apply these concepts, and integrate the learning into their own experience. Whether conducted in a threaded asynchronous discussion or through a live virtual interaction, the educator focuses on connection and engagement through discussion as a means to achieve course goals. Given the critical role of discussions in driving learning goals in an online course, discussions should make up, at a minimum, 20 percent of the total grade requirement for the course. Assigning a significant grade percentage of the final grade to discussions underscores the critical role of discussions in learning.

Use assignments to further learning. Assignments—or assessed learning tasks—require online learners to demonstrate deeper levels of learning by challenging them to integrate the concepts they learned from videos, readings, and discussions. Assignments can be as varied as the course goals themselves. The educator considers both the concepts, attitudes, and skills they want learners to acquire as well as the most engaging and meaningful way for learners to employ that new learning in completing the assignment.

The fourth goal of the Strategic Planning course is "By the end of this course, you will have analyzed organizations' internal and external environments to inform strategic objectives." In this course, class members engage in case studies throughout the course as a way to demonstrate understanding and critical thinking. With this goal, the educator challenges class members to analyze internal and external environments. The structure of a case study includes a framework that specifically requires this analysis.

The format of the assignment depends entirely on the course goals. Based on the overall topic of the course, the course could focus on effective communication with executive teams. Instead, the course goals primarily focus on critical analysis and creating effective strategies. For this reason, the educator could assign written projects rather than recorded presentations. Online educators can utilize virtually any type of assessment available in residential format, including reflections, research papers, presentations, quizzes, or tests. They must consider whether certain assignment formats are best for the online learner. Quizzes and tests, although a perfectly sound means of assessment, prove challenging when learners are not in a controlled environment with accountability measures in place to guard against the use of outside resources. After weighing all of these factors, ultimately, the learning goals determine the assignment best suited for deepening and demonstrating learning.

Online educators face a unique challenge when they consider the variety of assignments to incorporate, particularly in an accelerated course. Online learners are dependent on the clarity of the written assignment parameters to accomplish online learning tasks. Given the accelerated pace of the course, varying the assignments can distract class members from the desired learning. Instead, the online educator can establish predictable, consistent assignment expectations as a means for reducing confusion for the online learner. Although a variety of assignment types can be a helpful means for diversifying assessment, the online learner often benefits from an educator who prioritizes clarity and simplicity. The following table is an example of how an online course might distribute assignments toward a final grade:

Sample Grading Distribution Breakdown: Strategic Planning Course	
Activity/Assignments	Grade Percentage
Reading	0%
Videos/Live Sessions (4)	10%
Asynchronous Discussions (4)	20%
Case Studies (6)	40%
Summative Capstone Case Study	20%
Devotions/Reflections	10%
Total	100%

Pacing Online Learning

Online classes come in all shapes and sizes, depending on the program level and type. In the last decade, programs have increasingly accelerated online learning by reducing courses to more concentrated lengths. Rather than the traditional sixteen-week course spanning an entire semester and taken alongside several other courses, colleges and universities have opted for shorter, more concentrated online courses. By abbreviating online courses to ten weeks, eight weeks, or even six weeks, learners can still make reasonable progress in completing their program requirements without overlapping several courses. By taking courses in succession, they can focus on one or two courses at a time. Most online learners are somewhat older and have employment and family obligations that require careful balance with their educational goals. Abbreviated courses taken consecutively are an answer to this need for balance.

This accelerated pace for online courses, however, creates yet another challenge for the online educator: How is it possible to achieve the learning goals and workload requirements for a traditional sixteen-week course within a condensed time frame? The following table provides an example of a workload breakdown for an online course:

Sample Course Workload: Strategic Planning Course	
Activity/Assignments	Total Hours
Videos/Reading	48 hours
Live Sessions (4)	8 hours
Asynchronous Discussions (4)	12 hours
Case Studies (6)	36 hours
Summative Capstone Case Study	23 hours
Devotions/Reflections	8 hours
Total	135 hours

The federally-mandated minimum student workload for a three-credit course is 135 hours. In a sixteen-week course, class members would spend an average of eight or nine hours each week on learning activities, whether readings or assignments. For a residential course, class attendance often makes up a significant portion of this total workload. For an online course, the workload consists primarily of independent work in order to honor class members' need for flexibility. Condensing a three-credit course into eight weeks means that learners must allocate sixteen or seventeen hours per week to their studies. The following provides a helpful guide for how to balance workload for a course in eight-week format:

Sample Course Workload Breakdown: Strategic Planning Course							
Week	Videos/ Readings	Live Sessions	Asynchronous Discussions	Case Studies	Capstone Project	Devotions/ Reflections	Total Hours
1	6	2	—	6	—	1	15
2	6	—	3	6	—	1	16
3	6	2	—	6	—	1	15
4	6	—	3	6	—	1	16
5	6	2	—	6	—	1	15
6	6	—	3	6	3	1	19
7	6	2	—	—	10	1	19
8	6	—	3	—	10	1	20
Total	48	8	12	36	23	8	135

The table illustrates the challenge learners face in studying at an accelerated pace, but it also illustrates the challenge of pacing for educators. Balancing workload becomes an important consideration when teaching in the online format, particularly at an accelerated pace. Creating a reasonable and distributed workload for class members takes into account the learner's need for predictability. Online learners must often balance work commitments and family obligations. For that reason, a simple and predictable rhythm to the course is part of what makes the online modality possible for nontraditional learners.

Online educators who focus on learning will create a balanced approach to dividing the workload across the weeks of the course. Creating balance in the course might at times seem to conflict with the content of the course, but the online educator recognizes the needs of the learner and prioritizes learning accordingly. Although the content might drive toward a much heavier workload in the final weeks of the class, the online educator uses creative approaches to balance the load. Creating balance in the course does not mean sacrificing cumulative, capstone projects or papers. One strategy is to scaffold larger assignments to limit the impact of a heavier workload in the final weeks. The following table provides a possible example of a balanced workload in an eight-week course:

Sample Course Weekly Breakdown: Strategic Planning Course			
Week	Videos/Readings	Discussions	Assignments
1	Video: Welcome and Overview Readings: Intro and Module 1	Live Class Discussion	Case Study #1 (Sat)
2	Video: Key Concepts Readings: Module 2	Discussion Board #1 (Wed, Sat)	Case Study #2 (Sat)
3	Video: Applying Theory Readings: Module 3	Live Class Discussion	Case Study #3 (Sat)
4	Video: Best Practices Readings: Module 4	Discussion Board #2 (Wed, Sat)	Case Study #4 (Sat)
5	Video: Guest Expert Clip Readings: Module 5	Live Class Discussion	Case Study #5 (Sat)
6	Video: Advanced Topic Deep Dive Readings: Module 6	Discussion Board #3 (Wed, Sat)	Case Study #6 (Sat)
7	Video: Capstone Preparation Readings: Capstone Prep Readings	Live Class Discussion	Outline and Initial Draft of Comprehensive Case Study (Sat)
8	Video: None Readings: Reflection readings as needed	Discussion Board #4 (Wed, Sat)	Comprehensive Case Study (Sat) End-of-Course Survey (Extra Credit)

Best Practices for Online Instruction

The online educator's presence, discernment, and skill remain key elements for fostering learning in an online format. Online educators contextualize these elements to the online format. The primary goal in an online course is to demonstrate active presence in the course through proactive communication and responsiveness. The hope of every educator is that class members will be actively engaged in the course. Online educators set the tone by modeling the same behaviors that they want to see from their students. Educators communicate presence in a number of ways depending on the needs and expectations of learners. Here are seven best practices that help communicate presence:

1. Make contact early.
2. Communicate clearly and consistently.
3. Respond promptly.
4. Prioritize feedback and timeliness in grading.
5. Build community.
6. Make changes as necessary.
7. Aim for improvement.

Making contact early sets learners up for success by communicating availability, letting them know what to expect, and laying the foundation for a meaningful learning community. The goal is to communicate warmth and approachability. A brief survey and a welcome announcement are helpful strategies to make contact early.

A brief survey or learning needs assessment can help gain insight into the needs and expectations of class members. Asking class members about their former experience with the course material or their expectations and hopes for the course helps the educator contextualize approaches to communication and presence.

A welcome announcement establishes a tone and begins forming rapport with learners even before the class begins. A week before or at the start of a course, posting a welcome announcement or video, sending a welcome email, or hosting an optional live class session welcomes learners to the course.

Sample Course Welcome Announcement: Strategic Planning Course

Welcome to Strategic Planning! I am looking forward to working and interacting with you during this course. The course will officially begin on [course start date].

I love this course because it helps you connect what you have been learning about leadership and vision to successful execution. Effective leaders not only understand themselves, their teams, and their vision, but they have honed their skills in achieving results. We have all met leaders who seem to be all talk with very little real-world competence. We want to be leaders whot connect the work to the purpose—leaders who see the forest *and* the trees—and make sense of it all through effective strategic planning. I am looking forward to joining you in this process and honing these skills.

In week 1, remember to participate in the "Meet Your Classmates and Professor Video Introduction." I know that you all know each other already, but I am looking forward to getting to know you a bit!

Please remember that I am here to assist you in any way possible. Should you have any questions or concerns throughout the course, do not hesitate to reach out to me.

Ongoing communication will greatly reduce your stress and keep you moving forward in the course. Your success in this course and program is my goal!

Here is my contact information:
Instructor Email
Instructor Phone

Need to meet? Choose from my available times here:

Looking forward to a great course!
[Instructor Name]

Communicating clearly and consistently is an important component of being present in the courses. A detailed syllabus, good assessment rubrics, regular weekly announcements, and engaging email messages all work together to reinforce the goals for the course as well as the assignments that will help learners achieve those goals.

The syllabus for an online course often does more heavy lifting than a syllabus for a residential course. An online course syllabus should include a breakdown of every week of the course in greater detail than might be present in a residential course. The weekly summary in the syllabus reinforces the course schedule on the LMS. The goal is coherence and consistency throughout the course, using every medium possible. Including these details in the syllabus anticipates questions that might arise if learners miss an announcement or struggle to navigate the course.

Assessment rubrics also serve as helpful communication tools for the online educator. Rubrics complement assignment instructions by clarifying the specific expectations for each assignment. Using good rubrics reinforces the learning goals of the course and guides learners to those goals. Rubrics serve as another proactive way to communicate by using means and methods that are clear and accessible to online learners.

Weekly announcements create a regular pace for communication and reinforcement of the course schedule. Although the substance of the weekly announcement might seem redundant to information in the syllabus or listed in the weekly breakdown on the LMS, weekly announcements allow the educator to contextualize the learning of that week and reinforce motivation for the learners. Weekly announcements also deliver the instructions for the next week. For the less motivated class member or the student with less executive function, weekly announcements break down the course assignments into a manageable, week-at-a-time format to go directly to his or her inbox.

Sample Course Week Announcement: Strategic Planning Course
You made it to week 7! You are now in the home stretch! I would love not to have to take off any points for late submissions. Commit now to finishing these last two weeks strongly. In week 6, I hope that you found our conversation around corporate ethics a valuable one. Of all the topics that we cover in this course and in this program, your personal and professional ethics most define your leadership. In week 7, we will examine chapters 10 and 11 in our textbook. Chapter 10 examines the process of executing an organizational strategy, with an emphasis on converting a strategy into actions and good results for the organization. The chapter explores how executing strategy is an operations-driven activity that revolves around the management of people and business processes. Successfully executing a strategy depends on doing a good job of working with and through others, building and strengthening competitive capabilities, motivating and rewarding people in a strategy-supportive manner, and instilling a discipline of getting things done. Our case study will be Uber. It should be fun after last week's look at their challenging ethical/legal issues! Read the case and reply to the guiding questions by linking theories learned in the text so far. Make sure to answer the guiding questions by using all the content and models covered in our text up to this point. **Guiding questions [taken from assignment instructions and syllabus]:** Describe Uber's business model. What service is Uber providing to the market? Is its business model financially successful? How have Uber's successes and challenges measured against its competitors and other companies within the software industry? Using SWOT analysis, what are some examples of external and internal influences that have impacted Uber? What are Uber's options in handling California AB5, an attempt to reclassify Uber's drivers as employees? What potential impact would each decision have? Of the options discussed, what is Uber's best option to continue into the future? How does Uber's financial situation affect its decision-making process? Best to you as you come into this week! [Instructor Name]

    Engaging email messages are an important part of demonstrating presence in an online course. The goal of communication in an online course goes beyond communicating administrative details for the course. The educator is also attempting to demonstrate presence in the course, communicate warmth, and motivate learners to continue active engagement in the course. Usual standards for professional, business, and educational communication would be devoid of emojis, contractions, and excessive exclamation points. For the online educator, however, the rules are different. Since the goal is warmth and accessibility, class emails shift tone from the traditional, formal style of educational communication. Subject lines for emails become opportunities to connect and pique interest. An exclamation point becomes a helpful way to demonstrate enthusiasm and interest. A smiley face or emoji softens the tone to show approachability. To supplement in-person, in-class interactions, the online educator's communications aim to demonstrate care and interest in both the course and the student.

Responding promptly is essential to assuring class members that the educator is actively engaged and present in an online course. The online educator communicates presence to class members through response time and accessibility. In a traditional, in-person course, a learner can expect to ask a question during a class session or stop by a professor's office during office hours. In an online course, the educator must take extra care to replicate this same availability. The inherent risk to not replicating this availability is not only that class members feel disengaged or anxious, but also that they miss out on necessary information or guidance that would hinder their learning.

Particularly in an accelerated online course, where assignments are due more frequently and the workload is double that of a traditional course, timely response and access to the instructor are crucial to success. The educator should aim to respond within twenty-four hours of receiving an email message or a question through the LMS. Online educators should also make scheduling a virtual or phone meeting as simple as possible. They might choose to have specified office hours when they are available at a posted Teams, Zoom, or Google Meet link. Whatever tool or format the educator chooses for meeting with learners, the key is that there is intentionality in structuring and communicating availability.

Prioritizing feedback and timeliness in grading is another key way to demonstrate presence in an online course. In an online format, grading becomes a primary means of communication between the educator and learners. By providing detailed comments and notations on grading assignments, the educator values class members' work by showing careful review of that work. Grading feedback also creates learning opportunities by providing "feed-forward," so that learners receive actionable help for future work. The timeliness of grading and feedback is also significant for creating trust between the online learner and educator. Aim to grade any submission within one week of the assignment deadline. This discipline in grading will reinforce the educator's presence in the course as well as giving learners the opportunity to incorporate feedback into upcoming assignments.

Building community in an online course means that learners are connecting with the educator and with one another. It also facilitates active learning, because implementing learning tasks is still possible even in an online environment. Collaborative tools create opportunities for implementing learning tasks in online courses. Technology tools such as Google Docs, Slack, Microsoft Teams, Zoom breakout rooms, and Padlet allow educators to deploy strategies for group work and peer review. Using these tools models for learners what collaboration and open communication look like in the online environment.

Making necessary changes on the fly can be more challenging in an online course than in a residential course. In a classroom, the educator often recognizes and adjusts when learners are not grasping a concept or skill. Because online courses are carefully structured and built into an LMS, online educators might be tempted to remain rigidly committed to the design of the course rather than make changes, even when recognizing that class members need a change. That response would be a mistake, because online educators need to use the same adaptability and flexibility in the online environment as they would in a classroom.

For the online educator, making changes will often create a heavier administrative burden to adjust deadlines, modify discussion topics, and communicate with learners who might have already looked ahead in the course. The educator might also choose to increase the frequency of communication or make virtual office hours or discussions more frequent. If the educator recognizes that learning is not occurring or that there is confusion or frustration with the material, even in an online modality adaptability is essential. The online educator should take care to implement these changes thoughtfully so that they are not chaotic or overly disruptive for the class members. The effective online educator is attentive to the needs of learners and is willing to flex to ensure that learning is occurring.

Aiming for improvement means taking into account feedback from learners. The wise online educator creates frequent opportunities for learners to communicate their needs and concerns. Encouraging class members to identify strengths and weaknesses in the course allows the educator to adapt to the specific needs of class members. It can be frustrating to wait for feedback from students, only to find at the end of the course that it might have been possible to address those issues during the course. Rather than relying only on course evaluations, reaching out proactively to class members through anonymous surveys or with an email inviting constructive feedback is another way of being present in the course.

Given the limitations of course design resources and LMS support, implementing changes to an online course might be challenging. Online educators might be tempted to minimize changes each time they teach a course. Certainly, major changes and constant course revisions might not be possible depending on the resources of the university. Online educators can always look to improve how they deliver content through communication and grading feedback. They should make notes while teaching a course, reflect on feedback from class members during the course, and carefully review end-of-course evaluations. Reviewing these notes and incorporating changes, both small and large, can make all the difference in a course staying relevant and engaging for online learners.

As technology advances, dedicated educators will embrace new approaches and platforms as opportunities to support learning. Educators must continue to learn and grow, not only in their field or discipline but also as educators. Online learning offers new challenges and opportunities for learners and educators alike.

Conclusion

Online education is not going away. If anything, the online modality will continue to expand to accommodate the increasing number of nontraditional learners. Knowing that this modality is expanding, college and university educators should expect to engage in online education at some point in their careers, if not throughout their careers. Understanding online learning allows the educator to approach course development and course facilitation thoughtfully and in ways that mitigate the challenges and leverage the unique opportunities of online learning. Online learning illustrates how important it is for educators to recognize that they are also always learners. No matter the format of the course, educators are always looking for new ways to engage learners and foster learning. The online modality creates new opportunities to explore using existing and emerging technologies as powerful tools to enhance accessibility, engagement, and personalized learning experiences.

Food for Thought
What has been your own experience in online courses? What has been positive? What has been negative?
How are you communicating in email messages and announcements to an online class?
Which of these best practices can you implement or improve in your context?

Conclusion

Hopefully, the conversation that began in the introduction has been a thought-provoking and productive exchange with opportunities for reflection and deliberation that the Food for Thought questions seek to prompt. From this point forward, the focus shifts to application and implementation, as educators and educators-to-be begin to adopt and implement a learning-centered approach in their courses and classes.

Reviewing the Theory

The case for a learning-centered approach to designing courses, planning lessons, and delivering transformational higher education rests on the nature of interactive learning. Interactive learning has its challenges, but it also has benefits. Those benefits include an approach that is holistic, engaging, focused, developmental, integrative, collaborative, and reinforcing. It allows learners to take responsibility for their learning and so increase critical thinking, metacognition, content retention, and application to their lives and ministries.

A learning-centered approach understands that learners receive and process information differently. That understanding means that in order for learning to be effective, educators must know the individuals in their courses and classes. They must be aware of differences in emotion, motivation, cultural and social backgrounds, generational traits, and ways in which class members receive and process information. They must use multimodal approaches in course design and lesson planning that can improve motivation, engagement, and comprehension.

A learning-centered approach begins with course-level learning goals and works backward from those goals to other components of a course. Those other components—units, assignments, readings and resources, workload, and grade weighting—are all important, but their primary purpose is to assist learners in achieving the course goals. The focus of course design is on giving priority to learning, providing a structure and resources that facilitate learning, and assessing the degree to which transformative learning actually takes place.

A learning-centered approach uses the course syllabus as a multifunctional tool for communication, planning, motivation, and support. It keeps the focus on learning by setting the tone for the course, establishing clear expectations for the course, anticipating and answering questions about the course, reinforcing and clarifying the rhythm and flow of the course, and providing tips for success in the course. Effective educators also realize that—in order to remain relevant—syllabi will change as course goals and learners' needs change.

A learning-centered approach recognizes the importance of assessment in determining the extent to which class members are achieving lesson and course goals. Since a learning-centered approach begins with and focuses on learning goals, the third major question in defining a course is "What is the evidence that learners are meeting those goals?" After identifying the deliverables related to each goal, it is important to establish more specific criteria to assess achievement as well as levels of mastery related to each criterion. Well-designed rubrics reinforce learning goals, bring clarity to learning, and provide actionable feedback related to student progress.

A learning-centered approach aims for transformation in the lives of learners. Learning-centered lesson plans revolve around a memorable big idea and an overarching lesson goal. They target three domains of learning—content, character, and competence—and they aim to challenge class members on three levels of learning—information, appropriation, and transformation. A stair-step model for lesson planning uses three learning spaces to address different levels of learning as well as different domains of learning.

A learning-centered approach to instructional design emphasizes creating, implementing, and adapting learning tasks that increase student engagement, improve academic outcomes, and foster meaningful, transformative learning experiences in both the classroom and online environments. Weaving together thoughtful content and purposeful learning-centered strategies allows learners to gain knowledge, behaviors, and skills that not only change their academic development but also foster spiritual and emotional growth.

A learning-centered approach to delivering higher education explores existing and emerging technologies as powerful tools for both educators and learners to enhance accessibility, engagement, and personalized learning experiences. Understanding online learning allows the educator to approach course development and course facilitation thoughtfully and in ways that mitigate the challenges and leverage the unique opportunities of online learning. Learning-centered educators are always looking for new ways to engage learners and foster growth in content, character, and competence.

Putting the Theory into Practice

Viewed as a whole, the work involved in creating a fully learning-centered course with stair-step model plans for every lesson might appear to be overwhelming. If an educator has the time and energy to go revise every aspect of a course, it would be ideal to do so. If the time and energy are not available for total course overhaul, though, it is not necessary to do everything all at once. An incremental strategy can also be effective in working toward a learning-centered course.

For example, applying the concepts and guidelines in chapters 2 and 5 would be relatively easy steps toward a learning-centered course. Creating pre-class and/or first-day-of-class surveys would be relatively easy to do and would pay dividends in understanding the make-up of the learners in the class. If existing assignments do not have grading rubrics in place, developing rubrics for the most significant deliverables would be a manageable project.

Applying the concepts and guidelines in chapters 3 and 4 would take the process to the next level and would bring a course closer to a learning-centered model. Defining a course by beginning with the learning goals would involve more work, but it would focus the course on achieving those goals and would create greater unity and continuity within the course. Even if an institution has a standardized framework for course syllabi, it is usually possible to incorporate key elements of a learning-centered syllabus within that framework.

With a learning-centered course defined, applying the concepts and guidelines in chapters 6 and 7 to selected lessons within the course would be a good way to gain experience in alternative lesson planning and to field-test plans for a lesson or two. Implementing learning tasks in a lesson or two does not commit educators to converting an entire course. It does, however, provide valuable experience and feedback for future sessions. Both educators and class members might even discover that they actually enjoy interactive learning.

When it is necessary to convert a residential course to online delivery, the concepts and guidelines in chapter 8 will prove invaluable. Careful planning, effective implementation, and instructor communication will enhance the effectiveness of the course. Beyond creating brand-new online courses, adjusting existing online courses to a learning-centered approach allows online educators to meet learners' needs more effectively and to maximize available tools to support the learning process.

Answering the Basic Question

The basic question that educators and learners must consider is "What is the goal of education?" If the goal is to cover content, lecture will most likely suffice. If, however, the goal is learning, a more interactive approach is needed. If the goal is to meet personal preferences, educators will most likely teach as they were taught. If, however, the goal is learning, a multi-modal approach will be more effective. If the goal is to deliver information, an instructor-centered approach will be adequate. If, however, the goal is learning, a learning-centered approach holds greater promise.

The basic premise of this book has been that the goal of education is learning. From that perspective, therefore, the goal of education is to help learners experience holistic growth that transforms their thoughts, their attitudes, and their actions. A learning-centered approach to designing courses, planning lessons, and delivering higher education has its challenges, but it also has its benefits. The expectation is that, by adopting the blueprints set out in these pages, educators will find that the benefits far outweigh the challenges.

Appendix A

Course Definition Template			
Typical Learners			
Typical learners will be . . .			
Course Description			
In this course, you will . . .			
Course Goals			
By the end of this course, you will have		Domain	Level
1.			
2.			
3.			
4.			
5.			
Unit #1—			
Goals: By the end of this unit, you will have		Assignments	
1a			
1b			
1c			
Unit #2—			
Goals: By the end of this unit, you will have		Assignments	

2a	
2b	
2c	
Unit #3—	
Goals: By the end of this unit, you will have	Assignments
3a	
3b	
3c	
Unit #4—	
Goals: By the end of this unit, you will have	Assignments
4a	
4b	
4c	
Unit #5—	
Goals: By the end of this unit, you will have	Assignments
5a	
5b	
5c	
Readings and Resources	
You will need the following readings and resources for the course:	
Assignments, Workload, and Grade Weighting		
Total		

Appendix B

Workload Parameters		
Reading		
Highly complex	Many new concepts	10 pages per hour
Moderately complex	Some new concepts	12 pages per hour
Popular/Scripture	No new concepts	15 pages per hour
Writing		
Discussion forum	250 words per post	30 minutes
Journal/blog	250 words per entry	30 minutes
Reflection paper	250 words per page	30 minutes
Peer evaluation	250 words per page	45 minutes
Analysis paper	250 words per page	60 minutes
Research paper	250 words per page	75 minutes
Studying		
Vocabulary review	per word	5 minutes
Paradigm review	per paradigm	10 minutes
Pre-quiz studying	per quiz	60 minutes
Pre-exam studying	per exam	180 minutes
Testing		
Multiple choice quiz	per question	2 minutes
Short answer quiz	per question	5 minutes
Essay exam	per question	30 minutes
Language unit exam	per exam	90 minutes

Viewing		
Recorded lecture	per lecture	actual time
Narrated PowerPoint	per slide	actual time
Unnarrated PowerPoint	per slide	5 minutes
Tutorial	per tutorial	45 minutes

Appendix C

Syllabus Checklist	
Guiding Questions	**Checklist**
Communication	
Setting Clear Expectations • What policies are essential to a productive learning environment? • What policies are essential to student learning? • What policies are required by the college/university?	*Attendance* ☐ *Use of technology* ☐ *Plagiarism/academic integrity* ☐ *Artificial intelligence* ☐ *Late work* ☐
Focusing on Learning • How will this approach promote learning? • How will students understand or receive the material? • Can I add a visual (graphic, table, etc.) to communicate more effectively?	*Instructor contact information* ☐ *Course description* ☐ *Form and style guidelines* ☐ *Course workload* ☐ *Course evaluation* ☐ *Grading scale* ☐
Planning	
Connecting Objectives • Are the course objectives diversified in learning domains and levels? • How are the course objectives connected to program and career outcomes?	*Course objectives* ☐ *Course requirements* ☐
Structuring the Course • Does the course have a predictable rhythm? • Is workload distributed in the course?	*Course schedule* ☐ *Course workload* ☐

Motivation and Support		
Providing Resources • Are required course materials identified? • Are support services such as tutoring, writing centers, and mental health resources listed? • Are other readings and resources listed?	*Required course materials* *Resources* *Bibliography* *Office hours/contact information*	☐ ☐ ☐ ☐
Establishing Tone and Transparency • Have I considered how to inspire curiosity and a sense of purpose? • Are my tone and language inviting and supportive?	*Instructor welcome* *Personal introduction*	☐ ☐

Appendix D

Assessment Rubric Template					
Assignment: **Description:** **Purpose:**					
	Performance Level 1	Performance Level 2	Performance Level 3	Performance Level 4	Score
Criterion 1					
Criterion 2					
Criterion 3					
Criterion 4					
Criterion 5					
Comments:					Total

Appendix E

Lesson Plan Template	
Lesson Overview	
Course	
Instructor	
Topic	
Lesson Big Idea	
Lesson Goal	
Lesson ABOs and Learning Spaces	
Pre-Class Space	
In-Class Space	
Post-Class Space	
Pre-Class Learning Space	
Overview	
Goal(s)	
Resource(s)	
Task(s)	
Assessment	
In-Class Learning Space	
Overview	
Goal(s)	
Resource(s)	
Opening Stage Task	
Middle Stage Tasks	
Closing Stage Task	
Assessment	

Post-Class Learning Space	
Overview	
Goal(s)	
Resource(s)	
Task(s)	
Assessment	

Appendix F

THIS APPENDIX PROVIDES A supplemental list of learning-centered strategies. Each strategy includes a brief description and highlights what the task reinforces to promote meaningful learning.

- *Compare/Contrast*: Provide a Venn diagram and ask students to identify similarities and differences between two or more concepts using readings, discussions, or research, then discuss the findings as a class. Reinforces: analytical thinking, pattern recognition, and transfer of knowledge.

- *Community Service*: Assign a service-learning project that applies course content to a real community need. Include a reflection and debrief afterward. Reinforces: empathy and community mindfulness.

- *Concept or Mind Mapping*: Students create a visual diagram to show the relationship between key concepts. Reinforces: organization skills, visual learning, and retention.

- *Debates*: Structure formal arguments around a controversial issue with assigned roles or sides. Provide time for research before the scheduled debate and rebuttal. Reinforces: analytical reasoning and argumentative skills.

- *Error Analysis*: Students analyze erroneous examples of course content to identify and correct the errors. Reinforces: critical thinking skills, attention to detail, and evaluation skills.

- *Four Corners*: Pose a question, then ask students to move to one of four labeled corners of the room that aligns with their answer. Ask them to explain their choice. Reinforces: critical thinking, decision-making, physical engagement, and verbal skills.

- *Free Recall*: After a lecture, students write down everything they remember without looking at their notes. Allow three to five minutes of recall and then ask them to compare notes with peers. Reinforces: memory retrieval and self-assessment.

- *Learning Audit*: Ask students to reflect midway through the course on what they have learned so far or understand better. Reinforces: metacognition, ownership, and mastery of material.

- *Panel Discussion*: Select students to prepare short presentations on a topic while peers ask questions and offer feedback. Reinforces: synthesis of knowledge and communication skills.

- *Peer Critiquing*: Students review and give constructive feedback to classmates on assignments before turning in their work for a grade. Reinforces: constructive feedback, collaboration, and higher-order thinking.

- *Perspective Reversal*: Students prepare an argument for a position opposite their own view. Reinforces: empathy and deeper analytical skills.

- *Question-Based Lesson Plan*: Write two or three questions on the board to discuss at the beginning of class. End the lesson with the same questions to support learning. Reinforces: knowledge synthesis and reflective thinking.

- *Scavenger Hunt*: Divide students into groups to search for answers, examples, or key concepts based on the course material. Reinforces: logical reasoning, spatial awareness, teamwork, retention, and recall.

- *Seventh Inning Stretch*: Set a timer and give students two to three minutes to stretch, move, or listen to music. Reinforces: engagement through cognitive reset.

- *Socratic Questioning*: Use a sequence of guided open-ended questions to prompt critical thinking. Reinforces: critical thinking, inquiry, and reflective dialogue.

- *Summary Cards*: Students write a main idea or takeaway from the lesson on an index card. The instructor collects and reviews the cards for comprehension. Reinforces: recall and retention.

- *Symposium*: Students formally present individual or group research while peers provide feedback based on assignment rubrics. Reinforces: research, mastery, and presentation skills.

- *TAPPS (Talking Aloud Paired Problem Solving)*: Pairs talk through problem-solving aloud while a partner listens and asks clarifying questions. Reinforces: verbal reasoning, metacognition, collaboration, and problem-solving skills.

Appendix G

THIS LIST OF TECHNOLOGY tools for learning includes apps, platforms, and tech-based tools that support interactive and learning-centered instruction.

Tool Name and Website	Description
ABLConnect (Harvard) https://ablconnect.harvard.edu	Provides a list of active learning strategies by activity type, subject, and learning objective.
Blogger https://www.blogger.com	Blog platform for student reflection or journal assignments.
Canva for Education https://www.canva.com/education	Design platform for visual presentations (posters, slides, infographics).
ChatGPT https://chat.openai.com	AI-powered assistant as a support tool (brainstorm ideas, plan lessons, generate writing prompts, create rubrics).
Consensus https://consensus.app	AI-powered search engine that summarizes findings from academic research articles.
Drimify https://drimify.com	Creates educational games geared toward learning objectives.
SC Training https://training.safetyculture.com/	A mobile microlearning LMS to create, share, assess, and track educator training.
Edpuzzle https://edpuzzle.com	Turn videos into interactive lessons with embedded comprehension checks and tracking.
Elicit https://elicit.org	AI research assists in finding relevant papers, reviews, or summarizing content for academic writing.
Factile https://www.playfactile.com	Create interactive review games.
Gamma https://gamma.app	A presentation and document creation platform to transform outlines or text into slides.

Genially https://genial.ly	Create interactive visuals such as infographics, timelines, and escape rooms.
Google Forms https://forms.google.com	Create surveys, quizzes, and other forms for feedback collection or assessments.
H5P https://h5p.org	Create interactive content for video, presentations, and scenario-based learning.
Interacty https://interacty.me	Gamified participation with games, tests, quizzes, and other interactive tools.
Kahoot! https://kahoot.com	Game-based learning platform to create quizzes, flashcards, and interactive learning games.
Khanmigo (Khan Academy) https://www.khanmigo.ai/teachers	Create lesson plans, exit tickets, rubrics, and more.
Learnt.ai https://www.learnt.ai	Generates lesson objectives, assessments, and other support for instructional design.
Mentimeter https://www.mentimeter.com	Live polls, Q&A, word clouds, and quizzes during class.
Microsoft Forms https://forms.office.com	Survey, poll, and quiz tool integrated with Microsoft 365.
Miro https://miro.com	Presentation and collaborative whiteboard with flowcharts, diagrams, and mind maps.
Padlet https://padlet.com	Digital bulletin board for collaborative brainstorming, feedback, or sharing ideas.
Poll Everywhere https://www.polleverywhere.com	Live response system for polls, word clouds, and clickable images.
Puzzel https://puzzel.org	Customizable puzzle maker for reviewing terms and lesson content.
Quizlet https://quizlet.com	Online flashcard tool with practice tests, in-class games, and study guides.
Research Rabbit https://www.researchrabbit.ai	Academic literature mapping tool that finds relevant papers for academic writing.
Slido https://www.slido.com	Interactive Q&A, live polls, quizzes, and word clouds.
Socrative https://socrative.com	Formative assessment tool for real-time quizzes and exit tickets.
SurveyMonkey https://www.surveymonkey.com	Survey tools for course feedback, assessments, or research projects.
TED-Ed https://ed.ted.com	Short, animated educational videos with tools to create video-based lessons.

Top Hat https://tophat.com	Software for polls, quizzes, discussions, and course material delivery.
TriviaMaker https://triviamaker.com	Build trivia games to review content.
Wayground https://wayground.com	An online-based quiz and teaching tool for both classroom and individual.
Wooclap https://www.wooclap.com	Engages learners through interactive polls, quizzes, posting, and provides exportable reports.
WordPress https://wordpress.com	Blogging platform for students to publish essays, research, or reflections.
YouTube https://www.youtube.com	Online video platform for sharing lectures, tutorials, and curated playlists.

Appendix H

Bloom's Taxonomy (2001)		
Remember Bring an awareness of the concept to mind.	**Understand** Interpret or recall the information in a particular way.	**Apply** Use learned material in new and concrete situations.
<ul><li>Who...?</li><li>What...?</li><li>Where...?</li><li>When...?</li><li>Why...?</li><li>How much...?</li><li>How many...?</li><li>True or false?</li></ul>	<ul><li>How would you generalize...?</li><li>How would you express...?</li><li>What information can you infer from...?</li><li>What did you observe...?</li><li>What does this mean?</li><li>Choose the correct answer.</li><li>State in your own words.</li><li>Is this the same as...?</li><li>Give an example of...</li><li>Choose the best definition of...?</li><li>This represents...</li><li>Is it valid that...?</li><li>What seems likely? Show in a graph, table, chart, etc.</li><li>Which statements best support...?</li><li>What restrictions would you add?</li></ul>	<ul><li>How would you demonstrate...?</li><li>How would you present...?</li><li>Draw a story map.</li><li>Explain a character's decision-making process.</li><li>Do you know of another instance where...?</li><li>Can you group by characteristics such as...?</li><li>Which factors would you change if...?</li><li>What questions would you ask of this character...?</li><li>How would you change...?</li><li>How would you modify...?</li></ul>

Analyze	Evaluate	Create
Understanding the underlying structure of knowledge to be able to distinguish between fact and opinion.	Making judgments about the value of ideas, theories, items and materials.	Reorganizing concepts into new structures or patterns through generating, producing or planning.
<ul><li>How can you sort the different parts. . .?</li><li>What can you infer about. . .?</li><li>What ideas validate. . .?</li><li>How would you explain. . .?</li><li>Which persuasive technique is used?</li><li>Determine the point of view, bias, values, or underlying intent presented in the material.</li><li>If . . . happened, what might the ending have been?</li><li>How is . . . similar to . . .?</li><li>What do you see as other possible outcomes?</li><li>Why did . . . changes occur?</li><li>Can you explain the result of. . .?</li></ul>	<ul><li>What criteria would you use to assess. . .?</li><li>What sources could you use to verify. . .?</li><li>What information would you use to prioritize..?</li><li>What changes would you recommend to. . .?</li><li>Do you believe . . .?</li><li>How would you feel if . . .?</li><li>How effective are . . .?</li><li>What are the consequences of . . .?</li><li>What influence will . . . have on our lives?</li><li>What are the pros and cons of . . .?</li><li>Why is . . . of value? What are the alternatives?</li></ul>	<ul><li>What would happen if. . .?</li><li>List the ways you can. . .?</li><li>Can you brainstorm a list of new and unusual uses for . . .?</li><li>Can you develop a proposal that would . . .?</li><li>How would you test . . .?</li><li>Which alternatives would you suggest for. . .?</li><li>How else could you . . .?</li><li>Describe a rule or common understanding about. . .?</li><li>How would you design a plan to. . .?</li><li>What could you invent to..?</li><li>What changes would you make to revise. . .?</li></ul>

Bibliography

Alexander, Christopher, and James Sysko. "I'm Gen Y, I Love Feeling Entitled, and It Shows." *Academy of Educational Leadership Journal* 17 (2013) 127–31.

Anderson, Lorin, and David Krathwohl, eds. *A Taxonomy for Learning, Teaching, and Assessing: A Revision of Bloom's Taxonomy of Educational Objectives*. London: Pearson Education, 2014.

Armstrong, Robert, et al. *The Development and Evaluation of Behavioral Objectives*. Worthington, OH: Jones, 1970.

Bain, Ken. *What the Best College Teachers Do*. Cambridge: Harvard University Press, 2004.

Baker, Paul. *Integration of Abilities: Exercises for Creative Growth*. Anchorage, AK: Anchorage, 1977.

Barnes and Noble College. *Getting to Know Gen Z: Exploring Middle and High Schoolers' Expectations for Higher Education*. 2018. https://www.bncollege.com/wp-content/uploads/2018/09/Gen-Z-Report.pdf.

Bender, Tisha. *Discussion-Based Online Teaching to Enhance Student Learning: Theory, Practice, and Assessment*. 2nd ed. Sterling, VA: Stylus, 2012.

Bloom, Benjamin, ed. *Cognitive Domain*. Vol. 1 of *Taxonomy of Educational Objectives: The Classification of Educational Goals*. New York: McKay, 1956.

Bloom, Benjamin, et al. *Evaluation to Improve Learning*. New York: McGraw Hill, 1981.

Boettcher, Judith, and Rita-Marie Conrad. *The Online Teaching Survival Guide: Simple and Practical Pedagogical Tips*. 3rd ed. San Francisco: Jossey-Bass, 2021.

Bunce, Dianne, et al. "How Long Can Students Pay Attention in Class? A Study of Student Attention Decline Using Clickers." *Journal of Chemical Education* 87 (2010) 1438–43.

Camargo, Cristina, et al. "Online Learning and COVID-19: A Meta-Synthesis Analysis." *Clinics* 75 (2020) 1–4. https://doi.org/10.6061/clinics/2020/e2286.

Carr, Nicholas. "Is Google Making Us Stupid? What the Internet Is Doing to Our Brains." *Atlantic* (July/August 2008) 56–63.

Conrad, Rita-Marie, and J. Ana Donaldson. *Engaging the Online Learner: Activities and Resources for Creative Instruction*. San Francisco: Jossey-Bass, 2004.

Cross, K. Patricia. *Learning Is About Making Connections*. Cross Papers 3. Chandler, AZ: League for Innovation in the Community College, 1999.

Dehaene, Stanislas. *How We Learn: Why Brains Learn Better than Any Machine . . . For Now*. New York: Viking, 2020.

Dewey, John. *Experience and Education*. New York: Macmillan, 1938.

Digest of Education Statistics. "Table 311.22." IES: National Center for Education Statistics, June 2023. https://nces.ed.gov/programs/digest/d22/tables/dt22_311.22.asp?current=yes.

Dimock, Michael. "Defining Generations: Where Millennials End and Generation Z Begins." Pew Research Center. January 17, 2019. https://www.pewresearch.org/fact-tank/2019/01/17/where-millennials-end-and-generation-z-begins.

Eberly, Mary, et al. "The Syllabus as a Tool for Student-Centered Learning." *Journal of General Education* 50 (2001) 56–74.

Elmore, Tim, with Andrew McPeak. *Marching off the Map: Inspire Students to Navigate a Brand New World*. Atlanta: Poet Gardener, 2017.

Fang, Jing, et al. "Changes in Chinese Students' Academic Emotions after Examinations: Pride in Success, Shame in Failure, and Self-Loathing in Comparison." *British Journal of Educational Psychology* 93 (2023) 247–48.

Figueiredo, Michael. "Competency-Based Education and the Millennial Learner: A Perfect Pairing?" *Education Leadership Review of Doctoral Research* 11 (2023) 1–10.

Fink, L. Dee. *Creating Significant Learning Experiences: An Integrated Approach to Designing College Courses*. 2nd ed. San Francisco: Jossey-Bass, 2013.

———. *A Self-Directed Guide to Designing Courses for Significant Learning*. San Francisco: Jossey-Bass, 2003.

Fleming, Neil. *Teaching and Learning Styles: VARK Strategies*. Rev. ed. Christchurch, NZ: Self-published, 2005.

Gardner, Howard. *Frames of Mind: The Theory of Multiple Intelligences*. New York: Basic, 1983.

Gatta, Mary, et al. *Job Outlook 2024*. NACE, 2023. https://www.naceweb.org/docs/default-source/default-document-library/2023/publication/research-report/2024-nace-job-outlook.pdf?sfvrsn=57be133e_5.

Goodwin, Bryan, and Robert Marzano. *The New Classroom Instruction That Works: The Best Research-Based Strategies for Increasing Student Achievement*. Arlington, VA: Association for Supervision and Curriculum Development, 2022.

Goyal, Preeti, and Poornima Gupta. "Millennials in Higher Education: Do They Really Learn Differently." *Issues and Ideas in Education* 10 (2022) 1–12.

Graham, Donovan. *Teaching Redemptively: Bringing Grace and Truth into Your Classroom*. Colorado Springs: Purposeful Design, 2003.

Harrington, Christina, and Melissa Thomas. *Designing a Motivational Syllabus*. Sterling, VA: Stylus, 2018.

Jensen, Eric. *Brain-Based Learning: The New Paradigm of Teaching*. 2nd ed. Thousand Oaks, CA: Corwin, 2008.

Johnson, Aaron. *Excellent Online Teaching: Effective Strategies for a Successful Semester Online*. Self-published, 2013.

Katsampoxaki-Hodgetts, Kallia. "The 'Naked' Syllabus as a Model of Faculty Development: Is This the Missing Link in Higher Education?" *International Journal for Academic Development* 28 (2023) 451–67.

Kolb, Alice, and David Kolb. *The Experiential Educator: Principles and Practices of Experiential Learning*. Kaunakakai, HI: EBLS, 2017.

Krathwohl, David, et al. *Affective Domain*. Vol. 2 of *Taxonomy of Educational Objectives: The Classification of Educational Goals*. New York: Longman, 1981.

Kutscher, Martin, and Natalie Rosin. "Too Much Screen Time? When Your Child with ADHD Over-Connects to Technology." *Attention Magazine* (June 2015) 22–25.

Lakhani, Karim, and Robert Wolf. "Why Hackers Do What They Do: Understanding Motivation and Effort in Free/Open Source Software Projects." In *Perspectives on Free and Open Software*, edited by Joseph Feller et al., 3–22. Cambridge: MIT Press, 2005.

Lang, James M. *Distracted: Why Students Can't Focus and What You Can Do About It*. New York: Basic, 2020.

Lawson, Michael. *The Professor's Puzzle: Teaching in Christian Academics*. Nashville: B&H, 2015.

Leggins, Shanell. "The 'New' Nontraditional Students." *Journal of College Admission* 251 (2021) 34–39.

Levine, Arthur, and Diane Dean. *Generation on a Tightrope: A Portrait of Today's College Student*. 3rd ed. San Francisco: Jossey-Bass, 2012.

Lingenfelter, Judith, and Sherwood Lingenfelter. *Teaching Cross-Culturally: An Incarnational Model for Learning and Teaching*. Grand Rapids: Baker Academic, 2003.

Lowe, Stephen, and Mary Lowe. *Ecologies of Faith in a Digital Age: Spiritual Growth Through Online Education*. Downers Grove, IL: IVP Academic, 2018.

Marcis, John, et al. "A Survey of Faculty Views Regarding the Course Syllabus." *Journal of Accounting & Finance Research* 13 (2005) 185–91.

Marzano, Robert, et al. *Assessing Student Outcomes: Performance Assessment Using the Dimensions of Learning Model*. Alexandria, VA: Association for Supervision and Curriculum Development, 1993.

McKeachie, Wilbert, and Marilla Svinicki. *Teaching Tips*. 14th ed. Belmont, CA: Wadsworth, 2014.

Melisa, Rahyuni, et al. "Critical Thinking in the Age of AI: A Systematic Review of AI's Effects on Higher Education." *Educational Process* 14 (2025) 1–22.

Miller, Michelle. *Minds Online: Teaching Effectively with Technology*. Cambridge, MA: Harvard University Press, 2016.

Newton, Gary. *Heart-Deep Teaching: Engaging Students for Transformed Lives*. Nashville: B&H Academic, 2012.

Nilson, Linda. *The Graphic Syllabus and the Outcomes Map: Communicating Your Course*. San Francisco: Jossey-Bass, 2007.

———. *Teaching at Its Best: A Research-Based Resource for College Instructors*. 4th ed. San Francisco: Jossey-Bass, 2016.

Pashler, Harold, et al. "Learning Styles: Concepts and Evidence." *Psychological Science in the Public Interest* 9 (2008) 105–19.

Pellegrino, James, et al., eds. *Knowing What Students Know: The Science and Design of Educational Assessment*. Washington, DC: National Academies, 2001.

Pink, Daniel. *Drive: The Surprising Truth About What Motivates Us*. New York: Riverhead, 2009.

Plutarch. *De auditu*. In vol. 1 of *Moralia*, translated by Frank Cole Babbitt, 201–59. Loeb Classical Library 197. Cambridge: Harvard University Press, 1927.

Rabon, Melina. "Teaching Strategies to Assist Faculty in Effectively Engaging Gen Z Students in the Mastery of Course Content." EdD diss., Midwestern Baptist Theological Seminary, 2022.

Remenick, Lauren. "Services and Support for Nontraditional Students in Higher Education: A Historical Literature Review." *Journal of Adult and Continuing Education* 25 (2019) 113–30.

Richards, Lawrence. *You and Adults*. Chicago: Moody, 1974.

Riechmann, Sheryl, and Anthony Grasha. "A Rational Approach to Developing and Assessing the Construct Validity of a Student Learning Style Scales Instrument." *Journal of Psychology* 87 (1974) 213–23.

Seemiller, Corey, and Meghan Grace. *Generation Z Goes to College*. San Francisco: Jossey-Bass, 2016.

———. *Generation Z Learns: A Guide for Engaging Generation Z Students in Meaningful Learning*. Self-published, 2019.

Selke, Mary Goggins. *Rubric Assessment Goes to College: Objective, Comprehensive Evaluation of Student Work*. Lanham, MD: Rowman & Littlefield, 2013.

Sousa, David. *Engaging the Rewired Brain*. 2nd ed. Thousand Oaks, CA: Corwin, 2024.

———. *How the Brain Learns*. 3rd ed. Thousand Oaks, CA: Corwin, 2005.

Stevens, Danielle, and Antonia Levi. *Introduction to Rubrics*. 2nd ed. Sterling, VA: Stylus, 2013.

Strawser, Michael, ed. *Transformative Student Experiences in Higher Education: Meeting the Needs of the Twenty-First Century Student and the Modern Workplace*. Lanham, MD: Lexington, 2018.

Suskie, Linda. *Assessing Student Learning*. Hoboken, NJ: Wiley & Sons, 2018.

Talbert, Robert. *Flipped Learning*. Sterling, VA: Stylus, 2017.

Taylor, David, et al. "Transformation to Learning from a Distance [Version 1]." *MedEdPublish* 9 (2020). https://doi.org/10.15694/mep.2020.000076.1.

Taylor, George. "Emotional Engagement in Learning through Humor and Storytelling." *Pediatric Radiology* 50 (2020): 1352–53.

Taylor, Kathleen, and Catherine Marienau. *Facilitating Learning with the Adult Brain in Mind: A Conceptual and Practical Guide*. San Francisco: Jossey-Bass, 2016.

Twenge, Jean. *Generations: The Real Differences Between Gen Z, Millennials, Gen X, Boomers, and Silents—and What They Mean for America's Future*. New York: Atria, 2023.

———. *iGen: Why Today's Super-Connected Kids Are Growing up Less Rebellious, More Tolerant, Less Happy—and Completely Unprepared for Adulthood (And What That Means for the Rest of Us)*. New York: Atria, 2017.

Vella, Jane. *On Teaching and Learning: Putting the Principles and Practices of Dialogue Education into Action*. San Francisco: Jossey-Bass, 2008.

———. *Taking Learning to Task: Creative Strategies for Teaching Adults*. San Francisco: Jossey-Bass, 2001.

Wasley, Paula. "The Syllabus Becomes a Repository of Legalese." *Chronicle of Higher Education*, March 14, 2008. https://www.chronicle.com/article/the-syllabus-becomes-a-repository-of-legalese/.

Weichhart, Georg. "S-BPM Education on the Dalton Plan: An E-Learning Approach." *Communications in Computer and Information Science* 284 (2012) 181–93.

Wiggins, Grant, and Jay McTighe. *Understanding by Design*. 2nd ed. New York: Pearson, 2005.

Wilmer, Henry, et al. "Smartphones and Cognition: A Review of Research Exploring the Links Between Mobile Technology Habits and Cognitive Functioning." *Frontiers in Psychology* 8 (2017) 1–16.

Yount, William. *Created to Learn: A Christian Teacher's Introduction to Educational Psychology*. Nashville: B&H, 2010.

Zarra, Ernest. *The Entitled Generation: Helping Teachers Teach and Reach the Minds and Hearts of Generation Z*. Lanham, MD: Rowman & Littlefield, 2017.

Zull, James. *The Art of Changing the Brain: Enriching the Practice of Teaching by Exploring the Biology of Learning*. Sterling, VA: Stylus, 2002.

www.ingramcontent.com/pod-product-compliance
Lightning Source LLC
Chambersburg PA
CBHW060609230426
43670CB00011B/2044